Part-fiction and part-autobiographical, author Dene Lindley, captured the hearts, nostalgia and belly laughs of anyone daring (or wise enough) to obtain a copy of his first book, Unlucky Alf. The book was a success in the US, UK and even touched its toe on the continent of Australia.

But Alf Hart's story is far from over ...

If the 1960's was a tumultuous, free-wheeling era for a lad to grow up in the North of England, imagine going through the final stages of puberty in the disco-obsessed 1970's and 'early-girlie' 1980's ...

Other books by Dene Lindley:

Unlucky Alf

Alf's Curse

the continuing misadventures of a hapless Yorkshire lad ...

Dene Lindley

The Derwent Press
Derbyshire, England

Alf's Curse
By
Dene Lindley

ISBN: 978-1-84667-039-8

Book design by: Pam Marin-Kingsley, www.far-angel.com

Cover photo, back cover photo and author portrait by: Steve Place, Creative Images Photography
Email: info@creativeimagesphotography.co.uk

Published in 2009

by
The Derwent Press
Derbyshire, England

Dedicated to
Bluebell Wood Children's Hospice
and
The Rotherham Hospice

Best wishes

Acknowledgements

My special thanks go out to my wonderful supportive soul-mate Kate, and my super children Samantha and Marcus. Their help and encourage never fails to amaze me, and to this end I am eternally grateful.

I am lucky enough to have a brother who doesn't mind me ringing him at all hours requesting obscure information and sharing humorous anecdotes. Our friendship and closeness still remains rock-solid.

I addition I would like to thank Jo Lindley, Tracey Herring, David Yates, Chris Mapp, Sally Baum, Trish Kapur and Gervase Phinn for their genuine help and advice; Will Bush for his stimulating thoughts and creative thinking; Jerry Yates for his jokes and yarns of yesteryear; Matt Bulcroft for his patience and computer wizardry yet again; and my great friends Steve & Michelle Taylor, Roz Knox, Jean and Geoff Launders.

Kath Knight, Catherine and Keith Lee, all the staff at Rotherham Hospice, Philip Howard Books, the famous Amy Parkes, Phil Vincent, Brian and Sue from the Sitwell pub in Whiston, and Kim Hodgson for promotion and marketing.

Added extra thanks go to the brilliant Joti Bryant, the genius of Steve Place, the ultra cool Josh Hayselden, Allen 'Capri' Curbishley, and the faithful Pam Marin Kingsley.

Table of Contents

Chapter 1
Piles and Pylons

The depth of shit I found myself in had reached my chin and was still rising...

With tears streaming down my contorted face, body rigid and gripped by fear, and the wind howling like a demented Banshee, I asked myself the simple question: Why was I stuck at the top of a pylon in bleak mid-winter, precariously dangling from what seemed like several thousand feet up in the air, risking my young life. Up to the age of fourteen, my existence had been a collection of disasters and calamities. Never having 'Lady Luck' on my side, this time I had pushed the boundaries too far...

It was a miserable and mucky January morning in Maltby, South Yorkshire. The sky was pallid and death-grey, and the year was 1975. My bedroom windows were frosted over with a thick coating of ice, and the chilblains in my toes were burning like hell. I glanced over to my brown Timex watch, bought for me when I was seven years old for my first communion, and through blurred eyes, realised I'd overslept. It was six o'clock, and I should have met my Aunty Fanny at half past five on the quarry banking for a winter ramble. Oh shit!

I had recently celebrated, (well not exactly *celebrated*), my fourteenth birthday. My existence was following a steady downward spiral, but by now my coping strategies were getting better in dealing with life's crap. Fanny was only three years older than me, and my Mum's youngest sister. To me, she was more like an older sister than an aunt, and I looked up to her like an icon. She epitomised cool and chic, and what she said was *gospel* as far as I was concerned. She was a tomboy (hoyden) of the highest order, and hated anyone referring to her as a girl.

My grandmother and Fanny's mum had died young, so she had invariably been neglected by the rest of the family, who had all moved on emotionally. She was a spunky character who laughed in the face of adversity. She didn't believe in God, and was frightened of no one. It was Fanny who taught me about religion.

I recall her once telling me, "You better pray that stain will come out of your underpants Alf."

She was very grown-up for someone who was seventeen, and somewhat promiscuous, but to me she was just plain brilliant. I adored her.

I quickly jumped out of bed, scratched my nads, and dressed, not bothering to attend to my ablutions. I was late, and a bollocking was waiting for me. Slipping on my wellies, I leapt over our back fence, and raced towards the quarry, feeling excited and terrified at the same time. Under ominous skies, there stood one incongruous sight, surveying the terrain with a face like thunder. I was definitely in for a roasting.

"Where the chuffing hell have you been you worm?" she bellowed.

Trying to catch my breath and not tell her the truth, for fear of getting a clip around the ear hole, I responded by saying,

"I've been in a trance all night."

Please do not ask me why I should have uttered such verbal diarrhoea, but my brain was dead. Even to me, this retort sounded pathetic. Trite, even.

"I'll give you bloody trance you lying little shit," Fanny yelled, whacking me across the back of my head, (at least the blow hadn't been directed onto one of my ears, which by now blue with cold, and would have shattered into a million pieces on impact).

I had gotten away lightly, so I accepted the punishment with a humble, humiliated expression, and followed her into the quarry basin like a lap dog.

"If you are ever late for me again Alf, I will rip off your right arm and hit you with the soggy end," she said, glaring at me with her steely blue eyes.

Not daring to utter another limp excuse, I just looked down at the ground and trudged on.

Getting up at silly o'clock wasn't normally a problem for me. Sleep was an invasion of my play-time, and palling around with Fanny was one of the highlights of my miserable existence, so having been late made me feel even more downhearted.

"Cheer up you scrawny bugger and follow me. I've been watching a kestrel for over an hour, and I think I've spotted where its nest is." Pointing her finger straight out in front of her, indicating the nesting site, Fanny inadvertently stabbed me in the eye, causing me to wince with pain.

"Stop being a mardy arse, and dry your eyes. I need you to be able to see clearly, so you can shin up that pylon adjacent the quarry explosives hut," she bellowed.

A pylon; why did she want me to shin up an electric pylon? The fact that the bomb cabin sat underneath its metal legs, made me feel even more ill at ease. Glancing over towards the grey hollow skeleton pillar, I suddenly spotted the bird she'd been talking about, and my thoughts of imminent terror drifted off into the clouds with the soaring crow. It wasn't a bird of prey at all; but I'd learnt over the years never to question her on anything.

Fanny grabbed my coat collar, and yanked me back to reality.

"Look at the third arm of the pylon on the right hand side; follow to the end. What do you see Alfie-Boy?"

I felt like saying, "bugger-all," as my eyes were still smarting from the recent poke she'd given me. Not wanting to disappoint her by sounding stupid, I realised through watery eyes that housed be-tween the top limbs of the pylon was a bunch of twigs. I presumed this was indeed a kestrel's nest, but it was January, and the egging season was still several months away. What was I to do? Question her wisdom and authority of my sage and master, and mention this slight observation, or tackle the inevi-table climb to check out this old, abandoned nest? I plumped for the latter, and adeptly made my way skywards, not even bothering to discuss my futile and dangerous escapade. Fanny looked on in total satisfaction at my obedience, and nodded to me in approval. Oh well, at least I'd succeeded in making her happy, even though I was risking my life for absolutely nothing.

If you ever have the opportunity to climb a pylon, take it from me....DON'T! Not only is it extremely dangerous and stupid, it's also an extremely effective way of ending your life in an instant. These towers carry very high currents of electricity, which are lethal. They're also equipped with a barbed-wire skirt, approximately ten feet off the ground, to deter unauthorised climbers like me. These steel lattices are certainly not climbing frames for teenagers. Fanny, however, had differing views on this; so for me it was unfortunately onwards and upwards.

On a previous encounter at Granny Fart's orchard, I'd nearly surrendered one of my testicles, and here I was again, climbing over serrated wire with no form of protection. Miraculously, I escaped harm, and now I was facing the real test. Heading to the lofty heights of my new climbing frame, my heart started racing; my arms became heavy. God decided to throw in a good measure of nausea into the mix. I felt my face burning, and my wounded eye began streaming again.

"Get on with it you tosser," Fanny shouted, encouraging me along.

I was now sweating my tits off. I also felt like spewing up, but with my master down below, resembling Charles Manson and wielding a large stick, I pressed on.

"Get on with it Alf, and if you fall and break your legs, don't come running to me," Fanny said with a smirk. I always loved her logic.

Ignoring all the warning signs and laughing in the face of danger, I gingerly headed towards my goal—a bunch of rotted twigs. After several long and arduous minutes I was perched over the nest. The view from this vantage point was awe-inspiring; Fanny looked like an ant (well she was an aunt of sorts). I felt a tremendous sense of achievement. The fact that the nest was bare and the journey fruitless didn't dampen my spirits. Peering into the assortment of twigs and sticks, my eye was drawn to a sparkly object nestled in the base of the nest. On closer examination, I was surprised to see it was a gentleman's pocket watch. With the speed and dexterity of a pickpocket, I whisked up the loot, and tucked it into my jeans.

It was at this stage of the proceedings that I made the grave mistake of looking down. *Jesus*, I thought, the ground below seemed miles away. I was an excellent tree climber, but pylon shinning was in a different league. I was so focussed on getting to the nest, I hadn't realised how far I'd ascended. To make matters worse, I suddenly developed vertigo. Clinging to the cold metal for dear life, I froze with terror.

I instinctively closed my eyes, but this only made things worse; my imagination runs riot at the best of times. Oh shit, I thought. Now things really did look grim, even by my standards. Slowly and carefully, I inched my way along the steel limb of the pylon, until I reached its main structure. I then squeezed my arse tightly into the lattice framework with such force, I was instantly stuck—secure but stuck. Several hundred feet in the air, backside rammed like a cork in a bottle. What was I to do?

At this juncture, God decided to join in again and spice things up a little. The wind began to get up, followed by a fine rain, the sort that still manages to get you piss-wet through to the bone. To add further to my misfortune, I began to feel the penetrable icy cold of the pylon transferring directly through to my rump. Arses and cold surfaces are not a good combination. (I'm now certain that this was the birthplace of my haemorrhoid problem, which remained dormant for years, and is now wreaking havoc within my bumhole.)

Six chuffing hours I was stuck up that pylon, terrified, freezing, wet and utterly crestfallen. Finally I was aware of Fanny's presence. She had decided that leaving me there wasn't an option, so reluctantly she'd adeptly clambered the tower, and was now positioned behind me.

"Hold on tight with both hands for your life Alf," she barked her instructions up at me.

Gripping the hand/foot bars that protruded outwards from the pylon flanks, I felt the almighty force of her *Doc Martins* connecting with my rear, dislodging it from its resting place. Such was the relief, I almost completely let go.

As I gathered my thoughts together, Fanny decided to motivate me a little.

"Get yersen down there now, before I throw you off and kill you myself!"

On hearing these kind thoughtful words of encouragement, I quickly made my way down the steel tower—like a monkey on speed.

With feet now firmly on terra firma, Fanny looked deep into my eyes and clamped her strong hands on my shoulders. I was both trapped and mesmerised, and found myself taking part in a mindless staring competition. She dispensed with the Charles Manson look, now becoming more like a snake, about to sink its fangs into its prey.

"How many eggs, Sonny Jim?" Fanny said through gritted teeth, her mouth curling, and her eyes widening by the second.

It suddenly dawned on me that I'd have to enlighten her; the egg season was still several months away. But she hated being questioned in any way. She also despised being wrong, and the thought of my impending thrashing was now descending in a downwards motion from my brain to my trousers—motion being the operative word. Timing was vitally important, and quick as a flash, I whipped out the pocket watch I had retrieved from the nest.

Fanny was completely taken aback, and immediately released her grip of me. She stood there in front of me totally speechless, fascinated at her newly acquired booty. Her reptilian facial expression morphed back into something more humanlike, reminiscent of Ron Moody's Fagin in 'Oliver'.

"Good old Alfie-Boy; that's exactly what I wanted you to recover for me. But if you possessed a morsel of sense, you'd have realised that for starters, it's not egging season. Secondly, that's a crow's not a kestrels nest. And finally, if you'd have been paying more attention yesterday to Uncle Jack, when he informed us he'd recently stolen an expensive fob watch from Lazenbys, the jewellers on the High Street, and had hidden it in up in that particular pylon for safekeeping, you would have realised that you shouldn't have turned up at all this morning to meet me."

Not even bothering to try to fathom out Fanny's reasoning behind her latest scam, I could only say,

"What's a fob watch?"

"It's just like a pocket watch, but you have to fob someone off with a ridiculous tale to get hold of one," she retorted smugly.

Most, if not all readers will be wondering why a family member would steal a watch and hide it in an abandoned nest at the top of a pylon; and why another family member would concoct a sick scam to get a young boy to retrieve it. You must realise what kind of family I come from; our ancestors descended from pond life, and struggled to move on from this. The big break transpired when one of our forefathers slithered out of the water for a wash, and mated with a creature that was actually alive, and bingo. The family tree started branching out in whole new directions…

My Grandad told me we were related to the likes of Van Gogh, Genghis Khan, and Able, the famous rhesus monkey who flew into space in 1959. This pedigree helped create a whole new form of the human race; one which rarely fits in with society in general, but usually stays on the periphery. Grandad always said:

"Great intelligence and madness sit together like two kangaroos in a brothel, looking for hairs on their hands, and finding them."

My Grandad was as mad as his arse, as we used to say.

Getting back to the question of why someone would hide a timepiece so high up in an electricity pylon, I can only think that the pylon was used to 'watch' over unsuspecting idiots like me.

Chapter 2
Insomnia

Becoming a teenager presented me with a raft of problems, but trying to understand a woman, however young Fanny was at that time, took my reasoning and logic to new heights. Underneath her hard exterior I knew she liked me, (even though she rarely exhibited any form of affection towards me) but I could never comprehend why she always insisted in me pursuing dangerous stunts for her amusement. If the TV programme 'You've Been Framed' and camcorders had been around during the early '70s, Fanny would have been a millionaire twice over, just by videoing my humiliations. She would scream with laughter at my misfortunes, until she collapsed onto the floor in wild hysterics. I would just pick myself up and lamely smile back at her, such was my deep love. I was happy when she was happy; it was as simple as that.

As we made our way home from the pylon episode, Fanny suddenly stopped in her tracks. To attract my undivided attention, she whacked me across the back of my head; not a small clip, but more of a hammer blow. Credit to her it worked, and I stopped on the spot. After several minutes I had regained consciousness, and Fanny assisted me to my feet.

"What's up Fanny, what have you seen?" I said groggily.

Over the brow of the hill, directly in front of us was a massive hare, stood bolt upright. Fanny expertly whipped out her catapult and loaded it with a marble.

"Bob down Alf; don't you dare make a sound or I'll knock yer head off," she said.

Knock my bloody head off? Hadn't she just carried out a similar action on my cranium two minutes earlier? Were there no bounds to her correcting me?

Without any further questioning I ducked down, and jarred my knee. (Over the years, I've been a martyr to my patellas... God gave me knobbly knees made of fibreglass, completely useless when playing competitive sports, and of no use at all when praying!)

Wincing from the acute pain which was now shooting up into my chest, I fell backwards, and started a speedy descent into the bowels of the quarry basin. Quick as a flash, Fanny grabbed me by the foot and anchored herself to a nearby boulder, which pretty much saved my life. The drop from the crest of the hill was all of seventy feet, and littered on the quarry floor was a multitude of jagged rocks resembling broken teeth. With Herculean strength, she hauled me to safety. Before I could mumble words of sincere gratitude to my saviour, Fanny twisted my ear a full 180 degrees, so I could only hear things from behind me.

"You noisy little shit. You scared the hare off, just as I had it in my sights. That would have made good eating tonight. What's wrong with you Alf? You are always messing up," she said.

22

Once again I adopted the pathetic expression of a bound and gagged naked cretin, waiting to be spit roasted by his evil friends. In situations like these, I had learnt to say nothing, and hobbled off with my head down. We had moved no more than fifty yards when a flock of partridges, startled by our presence, flew up from our feet, making a noise which sounded similar to machine gun fire, only louder and more intense. The ferocity of their alarm calls and manic flapping of their short wings stunned me into complete shock. I was totally traumatised by this seemingly normal behaviour of game birds flying away from impending danger.

Partridges have a whirring flight, punctuated with gliding on downturned wings. They look like giant starlings when they are in flight. If they are flushed out of their habitat, they spit out a loud, high-pitched call, which degenerates into a rapid cackle: "*it-it-it*". When you're not expecting such a commotion, I can tell you it leaves you panic-stricken. I recall shaking violently and screaming. Fanny didn't fare much better. Even the mighty vixen-warrior was overtaken with fear. We both stood there rooted to the spot, not daring to move.

"What the hell was that?" Fanny said, still smarting from the experience.

"Red-tailed hawks," I replied.

We looked at each other with mouths still agape, and ran as fast as our legs could take us, which in my case was at tortoise speed. Eventually we arrived home. Fanny's parting order to me was to never mention what had just happened to any-one; not ever.

I wearily made my way into the living room, and collapsed on the sofa. I was still trembling three hours later, living the event over and over again in my mind. Terror grips people in different ways, and this was my first encounter with real fear. My next one followed five minutes later.

No one else was home that evening, so I flicked the television on. It was now half past ten, and 'Appointment with Fear' was on. The particular programme that night was the 1941 film 'Wolf Man', starring the brilliant Lon Chaney Jr. This was one of the classic films that inspired all other great monster horror movies. Normally I would have loved this flick, but after the firework partridges, I was scared shitless. The special effects in the '40s were rank, but I was totally taken in with Chaney's performance and was spellbound.

When the movie finally finished, I slowly turned towards the lounge door, only to be confronted by a large menacing shadow of a wolf on the wall. No words could describe how I felt at that second, but being brought up Catholic *Crikey Moses* would have sufficed. Riveted with terror, heart racing, sweat pouring, and bottom clenching, I reluctantly got to my feet, only to be attacked by our old dog Kesh.

"You nasty bastard, what are you trying to do to me?" I scolded my mutt.

Like most old curs, he completely ignored my protestations, and hobbled past me, due to his deafness and blindness.

I crept upstairs making spasmodic *Kung Fu* movements with my arms, just in case anyone tried to attack me from the landing. I was taking no chances tonight. I decided to skip washing and brushing my teeth, and clambered straight into bed with my clothes still on. I shut my eyes so tight it made my lip rise and expose my teeth, making me resemble what a Chinese man must look like whilst having a crap. I plunged under the covers and held my breath, hoping no one would notice me if they entered the bedroom. Not daring to move an inch, I lay there for what seemed like an eternity. My heart was beating so loudly, the vibrating went right through the mattress. I didn't sleep one wink that night; I just stayed under the covers, rigid with fright. This was my introduction to insomnia.

INSOMNIA

Insomnia is a sleeping disorder characterised by a persistent difficulty in dropping off to sleep. Insomniacs have been known to complain about not being able to close their eyes, or rest their minds for more than a few minutes. I've spent bloody hours wide awake at night thinking this through, all to no avail. There are at least three types of insomnia that exist: acute, chronic and transient. I have all three in varying degrees, but my favourite by a country mile is chronic.

My insomnia manifests itself in me being wide awake. I often sleepwalk, or shout out in the middle of the night for no apparent reason. I occasionally can switch off, but it all depends on how many other people are inside my head at any particular moment. I once tried telling all the inhabitants of my brain the same story at the same time, but several of them started a debate about windsurfing, so it all went tits up.

Not being able to sleep properly can and does affect a person when they are awake, due to fatigue and stress. Depression is a great friend of insomnia; they get on brilliantly. I know. I have both. A common misconception about insomniacs is that the amount of sleep a person requires decreases as one gets older. Complete bollocks, believe me; I am permanently knackered.

The only real cure for insomnia is sleep. I personally use organic mind-bending drugs. It doesn't help me sleep, but the hallucinations are top notch. I know it's not big or clever, and I don't purport to know all the answers, but magic mushrooms are my remedy, and they are in fact legal. I grow my own in my soiled under-crackers in our cellar. They are exquisite with sausage and brown sauce sandwiches, or delicately pan-fried and used as a topping on Asda's pizzas. Jamie Oliver doesn't know all the tricks, my friends.

Remedies to combat sleep deprivation include drinking warm milk before you retire to bed. I've tried this and it was rubbish, so I opted for a bottle of red wine. This also proves to be ineffectual, but tastes shitloads better. Another idea is exercising vigorously at the gym in the afternoon. The only energetic exercise I do in the gym on an afternoon is in the communal steam room—enough said.

In the Buddhist community, people who struggle to sleep are advised to meditate. Have you ever tried to meditate? I've tried this technique hundreds of times but it has never worked for me. My advice is stick to the drink and drugs. It doesn't aid the sleeping, but does make you feel warm on the outside, and cooks your brain from the inside.

Visualisation can also be effective in transporting the mind away from present day problems and anxieties and towards a more peaceful state of mind. This is another disaster for me, as I never get beyond the thought of women with enormous tits.

I often think about the dyslexic, agnostic insomniac, who stayed up all night wondering if Dog exists?

Chapter 3
On the Buses

Now blessed with my new friend insomnia, life took a turn for the worse. I found that I couldn't sleep at all during the night, but come daylight hours, especially during school lessons, I craved it like the popular dessert *Death by Chocolate*. I never liked school at all. Not one jot.

My brother Craig and I made the unfortunate mistake of passing our 'Eleven-Plus' exam in the top class at St. Marys, and ended up going to De La Salle College, which was situated in Sheffield some 12 miles away. To compound matters, when I realised I had been accepted into this establishment, my mother mentioned the fact that my first two years there would be spent at a satellite school based in Beauchief, which was a further five miles, and another bus journey. I hated buses with a passion for one reason; having to be in such close proximity to other kids. Oh, and travel sickness.

If I had realised that passing the exam would have put me through the torture of having to attend another Catholic school with mad monks in charge, having to get up one hour before all my mates just to get there, arriving home one hour later than them, and being subjected to even more prejudice than at primary school, I would have flunked it big time or in some style.

THE ELEVEN PLUS

The 'Eleven Plus' examination was administered to children in their last year of primary education, and was used to determine which type of school the student should attend upon leaving. This could be a college, grammar or secondary modern. It was intended to establish a Tripartite System of education, with an academic, technical, and functional strand. The only thing I knew about the Tripartite System was that it was used in South Africa, and caused great bloodshed and discrimination between the blacks and the whites of the population.

I was also told that the 'Eleven Plus' was created by the 1944 Butler Education Act. During the '70s, Maltby was overrun with Butler lorries transporting stone from the nearby quarry at Stainton. Why this popular haulage firm had previously got involved in education still baffles me to this day!

The Education Authority at that time thought this system was an effective way of identifying which particular school each individual child was most suited to. It also became fiercely competitive and quite elitist for the successful students. Six pupils passed the exam in my year, and we were made to pay for our intelligence by both the Protestants who already hated us, and our own classmates who had subsequently failed it. We became known to all and sundry as *Racing Snake's Bellies*, something you can't get lower than.

Our school and church thought it magnificent that we had been accepted to a college, but looking back on the whole debacle of me attending

De La Salle, and the complete misery it bestowed upon me, I should have deliberately failed that test. Sometimes, pleasing the wrong people, and not pleasing yourself, can have traumatic consequences, especially in later life.

During the '60s and early '70s, the authority of parents and teachers alike was being undermined in a way that was unprecedented. Everything old-fashioned, traditional and customary was being replaced. Children were being told to challenge authority, stand up against parents' morals and beliefs, and pretty much do as they wanted by their peer groups. Not at our chuffing school! Discipline was always the order of the day, followed by more discipline, and masses of homework. Religion was not classed as outdated like it is with today's teenagers, and having morals meant something to a person. I was never allowed to express myself, unless it was within the confines of the bathroom with one of my uncle's magazines.

As if school wasn't bad enough, the journey there was a nightmare—even though it was during daylight hours. Mum would drag me and Craig from our warm pits, shovel a morsel of food into our mouths, and off we'd go, occasionally neglecting to wash or brush our teeth. We must have looked a right set of scruffy buggers. Racing to the corner of our street, we would meet up with a guy called Piggy. This lad was a legend; Craig and I looked up to him, even though he was smaller than us both. He was as bright as a button and as sharp as a sixpence. Piggy would greet us by swinging his leather briefcase around, and belting either one of us in the side of the head. It was just his way of saying good morning.

All three of us would then sprint to the foot of Addison Road and await our antiquated form of transport, which in this case was a dilapidated red double-decker bus. Most other school children in Maltby would still be in their beds, due to the fact that the local comprehensive was on everyone's doorstep. We, however, had to make the arduous trek over to Sheffield, then beyond to Beauchief, taking at least one and quarter hours. It was purgatory, believe me.

Double-deckers had a tendency to get less crowded than the average charabanc. To the rear of the first level of the bus, it had seats facing each other, designed for a more convivial atmosphere than the standard rows. Each child was allocated a specific seat on the bus; mine was on this three-seater, looking directly across to three other glum mugs. When the bus did get crowded, you would end up bumping knees with other kids who were unfortunate enough to have to stand up during the ride. The one thing that all kids did who sat on these inwardly facing seats was to adopt a fixed stare straight ahead, never flinching or daring to glance sideways, for fear of attack or ridicule from other passengers. In my early days travelling through to Sheffield, I often endured such a lambasting from my so-called pals.

During the journey home one evening, I found myself nodding off to the throb of the bus, whilst it sat waiting at the traffic lights in Brinsworth. The outside world was now cloaked in blackness, and, coupled with the warmth generated by my classmates, I found myself succumbing to slumber big time. You may have experienced this state yourselves, especially when you are sat upright in company, pretending to be interested in what they are saying. You unexpectedly begin to drift off into oblivion, sporting a gormless expression, with your eyelids cascading in a downwards motion, never wanting to open again. Just prior to nodding off completely, your head starts to feel like a giant cannon ball balancing on a pin. With one wrong move or sudden jerk, it snaps and is thrust forwards in a violent movement, startling you and all around you. My particular trick was to throw in terrifying sound effects, just at the moment my head disconnects from my shoulders; this was for added theatre, according to my brother.

With a resounding squeal and a massive jolt to the back of my neck, I found myself surrounded by children laughing and pointing to my trousers. Still half dazed, I had no idea why so many kids had packed into the rear of the bus, and were now virtually falling over me, howling with mirth and mocking me mercilessly. It didn't take too long to realise what all the fuss was about. Unbeknown to me, with the vibration of the bus gently rocking my legs and body and my mind elsewhere, I had unwittingly produced an erection in my pants for the ensemble around me. To compound matters even further, my zipper had inadvertently come down, and my pocket-rocket was thrusting my vivid red underpants beyond their normal confines, and into plain sight, for all to admire. What a complete arse

I felt when this devastating incident eventually registered with the old grey matter.

Quick as a flash, I clasped my zipper, and tried to force it shut to cage the wee beastie. No such luck. My bell-end got caught in the zip, and blood oozed everywhere. What was I to do? Everyone was by now screaming hysterically at my misfortune, such was their genuine care for my health and welfare. With gritted teeth, I yanked the zipper down to release my frilly, yet bloodied winkle. With careful aplomb, I managed to get *the boys back in the barracks*, even though the *general* was well and truly wounded. There's a lot to be said for leading from the front!

It took me weeks to get over my hapless misfortune, and just when I thought things were beginning to get better, lightning struck again. I sat in the middle of the three-seater, with my mate Bogger on my right and Dougie on my left. Directly behind us was situated a two-seater, and then the back seat, which housed five people. One evening, another bus broke down, so ours was seconded to pick up extra passengers for the homeward journey. To my great delight, the travellers were all sixth-form girls from a neighbouring school in Sheffield. With legs up to their arm pits, and fulsome bosoms, my tiny mind went into overdrive. Even though we were to be graced with such beauty and elegance, my manners went straight out of the window, along with all my chums, because there was no way we were going to give up our seats to girls.

A prefect named Jed tried to intervene, and act in a chivalrous and dignified manner, by requesting that the 'three-seaters' stood up to make way for the young ladies. A deafening "Bollocks!" echoed around the bus. Failing in his first attempt with the third-year pupils, he opted for the easier and softer target of the first-year boys, or *Fags*, as they were referred to. Credit to these little imps, they put up a reasonable fight, until another prefect got involved and booked all five of them. Like the cat that got the cream, Jed smugly escorted his five belles to the back seat. As if this wasn't bad enough, he whipped out his handkerchief, and pretended to dust down the crumbly scarlet leather for their comfort. Well you can imagine how thrilled the girls were at this magnificent act of gallantry. Me and the lads thought it pathetic, but said nothing to avoid being booked, and dragged in front of the headmaster.

As the bus pulled away from the girls' school, all the 'three-seaters' began the daily mindless front-faced staring competition. On this occasion however, our necks were straining to peer to the rear of the bus to admire and fantasise about the chicks. We had managed to travel approximately five miles, when Dougie grabbed my right wrist and said,

"Alf, don't look until I give you the command, but the girl who is sat in the middle of the back seat has got no knickers on and you can see her spider's legs."

Jesus wept, I thought. There is a God, and tonight his blessing is on me. Trying not to attract undue attention, and simultaneously trying to swivel my head like an owl, Dougie gripped me even tighter.

"Not until I give you the command, mate!" he said.

The suspense was killing me, and as so often happens to pubescent boys, my penis decided to pop his head up so he could get an eyeful. I must tell you here and now, inwardly facing seats on double-decker buses leave no room for concealment, when it comes to getting an erection. Having been previously caught out with this just a few weeks earlier, so I quickly instructed my mind to think about something less sexually arousing, like the inside of a football, or the Pope. Brilliant; it seemed to be working, and my member began to subside.

"Hey Alfie, are you ready? When I give the signal, lean forwards and have a good ogle pal," Dougie whispered in my ear hole.

The tension was now at bursting point, and just when I thought that I couldn't restrain myself any more, Dougie gave me the signal. I lunged forward and twisted my head to the right, whilst still remaining seated, but with my torso bent at ninety degrees, facing the intended vision of beauty. Looking like a deformed *wooden top,* complete with perverse expression, I locked my eyes in the region of the girl's muff with radar accuracy. With mouth agog I focused my vision with all its might, squinting in the process. It was at this stage of the proceedings that it all went pear-shaped.

Dougie, being the callous and vindictive bastard he was, turned his head to his left to face me, and with the dexterity of an accomplished ventriloquist, said out loud for all to hear, "Hey goolie-gobbler, look at me looking up your skirt."

Everyone, including the girl in question, fixed their eyes on me. Needless to say, the girl did have knickers on, and here was I, bent double, ogling her growler for a cheap thrill. She stood up, stormed over to me, and kneed me in the nose. With blood everywhere, and the world and its dog laughing their respective tits off at me again, when would I ever learn?

Another lasting memory from my teenage days relates to my friend Piggy. Being a small rotund lad with a mischievous streak, he was forever getting into altercations with other kids. He seemed to enjoy baiting and tormenting them relentlessly, such was his nature. Piggy was from a more affluent family than Craig and I, but didn't judge us like the rest of our school. He seemed to understand that our impecunious situation was nothing at all to do with us. He would often taunt me with: "Old Alfie-Boy; hasn't got two pennies to scratch his arse".

I remember him telling me about the new continental quilt his mum had bought him for the new divan. I hadn't a clue what he was talking about until he explained he had acquired a new bed and eider-down. Craig and I slept together under the warmth of my Grandad's trench coat. It did keep you snug, but itched like mad, and often snagged our vests. (Later on, good quality quilts with their respective tog values would have been wasted on me, as an early lifetime of frugality had left me incapable of enjoying any form of comfort.)

Every evening as Craig and I disembarked from the bus, our so-called mate Bogger would slide open a small window vent, and spit at us—such was his friendship. This he did every night, without fail. We would end up festooned in his goss, not being able to defend ourselves. This however didn't happen when Piggy was accompanying the pair of us. Piggy could have represented Great Britain when it came to spitting; such was his accuracy and speed. Piggy could clear the width of a main road from a standing position, and taught Craig and I to spit by flicking our tongues. I personally perfected this technique in church, and managed to cover the back of my aunt's hairdo with tiny bobbles of saliva.

On one particular evening, Craig and I leapt off the bus, and braced ourselves for the spittle onslaught. Bogger took up his usual position, and we quickly pulled up our hoods for protection. The bus window opened slightly, not much more than a gnat's arse and Bogger readied himself. Suddenly in a flash, Piggy appeared from behind the adjacent bus shelter, and gazelle-like leapt up in front of Bogger's glass protection. I can still see the reflection of Piggy's face, etched with menace, and revenge written all over it. *Whoosh.* Piggy expelled his secretion into the cold night air, and through the smallest of cracks, it whizzed its way like a torpedo, straight through the nick of the window, and landed directly into Bogger's mouth. Bang on target, and with monumental consequences. As the bus pulled away, we all stood in total joy as Bogger was seen spewing up over his fellow passengers.

In 1969, a TV comedy series began called 'On The Buses'. It was based around the relationship of a bus driver and conductor working on the No 11 bus that ran to the cemetery gates, in London.

The main cast was comprised of a happy-go-lucky bus driver Stan Butler, his mate the lecherous conductor Jack, and their boss, Inspector Blakey. What made this sitcom so funny was the interaction between the driver Stan Butler and Blakey. Blakey's catchphrase was: "I 'ate you Butler!"

This struck a chord with me, as the guy who created the 'Eleven Plus' was called Butler, and I hated him!

Chapter 4
Camping it up with the Boys

Being in the cubs was an excellent grounding for joining the scouts. I chose however to have a long career break, after leaving the cubs at eight years old, before joining the 12th Maltby Gaylords at fourteen and a half. It was a sort of sabbatical for me, allowing my mind to readjust to reality. Being part of an all boys outfit, however young, can have a traumatic effect on a young kid's mind. They say "boys will be boys," but occasionally boys jump ship and stray over the gender barrier. Being in the boy scouts was a splendid accelerant to this transition. I am an open-mined person, and being part of a pack of pubescent teenagers, I needed to be.

I was part of a patrol called the 'Cockatoos', and my patrol leader was a lad named Larry. He was sixteen years old and ready to leave the scouts and join the venture scouts, which was a big move up to being a fully fledged leader. He was a fat lad with round National Health spectacles, tied together with an elastic band so they wouldn't fall off his head. He was an effeminate sort of youth who persisted in tapping you on the rear at every opportunity. If you did something wrong he would slap your arse, and if you did something right he'd gently tap it, twenty times or more.

The one thing I loved about being in the scouts was the different badges you could achieve from your basic 'Scouts Standard', through to your 'Advanced Scout Standard', and finally the 'Queen's Scout Award'. I managed to get my head down throughout my short, illustrious scouting career and bagged all three in record time, which was somewhat of an achievement for me. My mates Potter, Joker and Dougie, all earned the same honour; we were only the second batch of boys to reach such a high standard.

On the whole Larry was a nice kid. He was, however, obsessed with cleanliness and was forever tidying up around us, especially on camp-sites.

Each year a bunch of scouts from each troop was chosen to take part in a competition at Hesley Wood in Chapletown, on the outskirts of Sheffield. As 1975 drew to a close, I was chosen along with our patrol to represent Maltby Gaylords. The competition was over two days and affectionately referred to as the 'Arab Shield'. It involved numerous activities, ranging from canoeing through to building rope bridges. I loved the outdoor life, and revelled in building things from natural materials. I was in my element in the woods; I always will be.

Hesley Wood is only twelve miles from Maltby, but it might as well have been in a different country. Even as a teenager I had no perception of just how far places were in relationship to my home town. The only thing that concerned me was beating the other troops from Maltby. The rivalry between the other local scout troops was fierce. I can only liken it to the local derby football matches when

Sheffield Wednesday take on Sheffield United; the hatred, sectarian undercurrents and will to win at all costs take over. The *bragging rights* after the game are savoured by the victors, and ridicule and humiliation is heaped upon the losers until the return match, which in our case was another twelve months away.

Unlike football, the competition we were involved in had a multiplicity of games, including obstacle courses, mental tests, canoeing, abseiling and camping techniques. Our team consisted of six members of our pack. We were chosen not because of our special skills, but basically, no one else in the platoon gave a shit about it. Personally, I was delighted to represent the 'Gaylords' and relished the challenges that lay ahead.

Larry was put in charge, and we assembled outside the market stalls adjacent the Catholic Club one Friday evening, bags packed and stolen booze well concealed in the base of our rucksacks. It was a pre-requisite to sneak alcohol into camp; all the young boys did it. My choice of fire-water was always 'Kestrel Lager', which was cheap and slightly more drinkable than Potter's Irish moonshine known as 'Potcheen', which was reputedly made from potatoes, and could strip paint and fuel a car. Potter's dad used to smuggle it over from Tyrone, Ireland in a plastic pop bottle, whenever he brought his disabled grandmother over from Ireland to the mainland. The customs guys always used to check the Catholics for it back then, but being the Irish equivalent of a female 'Ironside', she was never frisked.

For a young lad, Potter could sink a dram or three, which was quite a feat for someone so small. I only tried it the once, and was violently sick. I also vaguely remember seeing hundreds of Leprechauns and money spiders, but I'll share that particular experience with you on another day. Needless to say, I had what the Irish describe as the 'craic'—right across the back of my head from our local priest at the time, rendering me unconscious.

Thirty minutes after setting off, we arrived at our intended destination and pitched camp. Joker got a fire started, and Larry commenced cooking supper. I had other things on my mind, like carrying out a full and comprehensive surveillance of the entire campsite, to pinpoint our bitter enemies from Maltby, and locate their precise positions.

It had now begun to get dark so mapping out the terrain was vitally important to us. We needed to know exactly where our fellow competitors were sleeping, so as to disturb them at frequent intervals throughout the night. As luck would have it they were camped ten feet away from us on either side of our tent; the 'Cliff-Hills Clowns' on one side, and the 'Crag-Bags' on the other. My one hour of reconnaissance turned out to be a complete waste of time.

On the plus side, our foes were close enough to easily get at, without having to traipse around the rest of the site in the middle of the night, searching for them in complete darkness. The 'Clowns' and the 'Bags' didn't even acknowledge our presence, but made it strikingly obvious to us that they were as thick as thieves. They swapped stories with each other, laughed and joked aloud, about how they were going to whip our hides in the competition, and made reference to the fact that we were the poor relations of Maltby in every sense of the word.

Looking at the state of our tent, peppered with holes, and falling to pieces, we did look a pathetic lot. Our scout master had dumped us and our decrepit tackle at the campsite gates, and pissed off home as quickly as possible so he didn't miss opening time at the Catholic Club. Our adversaries had been transported in a coach catering for all their needs, including bringing their parents with them for moral support. These adults would be staying in the lodges next to the tuck shop adjacent the main entrance.

To me, the whole idea about camping was being away from your parents; these wet-lettuces had brought their mummies and daddies along with them to assist in cooking, cleaning, washing up and cheering from the sidelines. Our parents didn't give a fuck about supporting us. If I remember rightly, my mum didn't even know I had gone camping for the weekend such was her lack of interest in me. One thing that did piss me off about the other scouts from Maltby was the fact that their parsimony and selfishness had stopped them asking us if we wanted a lift to Hesley Wood. Their coach was half empty when it arrived and seemed somewhat wasteful to me. All this did was fuel my hatred for them.

At ten o'clock it was lights out, and all competitors retired to their respective tents for the

evening, snuggling into their sleeping bags, looking forward to a wonderful night's sleep. A muffled
silence descended over the campsite, and fiend-
ish plans began to take shape, in our case under
cover of rotting canvas. Such was my intense anger
at my neighbouring fellow scouts, I was intent in
causing as much damage and disturbance as one
youth could.

My first port of call was with the 'Bags' tent.
In my infinite wisdom, I took it on myself to set
fire to the tent sides. Within seconds it was ablaze.
I alerted the occupants, by dragging them out by
their sleeping bags, whilst simultaneously throwing vast fire-buckets of water over the flames. This
act of brilliance extinguished the flames, soaked the
inhabitants, and thoroughly destroyed their tent.

Having successfully retrieved all the scouts
from their canvas shelter, I had the brazen audacity to accuse them of being totally irresponsible
for not dousing their fire prior to them retiring to
bed. Obviously, a stray spark had ignited the tent.
I admonished them for their lack of responsibility
and said I would be reporting them all to the camp
commandant the following morning. It was marvellous to see them standing there, sobbing into their
pyjamas at this scene of destruction. Looking back
on this sorry incident, I realise how foolish and
featherbrained I'd been for starting what could have
been a fatal fire. This was arson at the very least,
and could have led to murder charges. But in my
defence, in my demented logic, they should have
let us ride with them on the coach in the first place,
and then none of this would have happened.

My next act of vandalism that night involved even more firepower. When the entire calamity had calmed down, and the 'Bags' had been re-housed with their parents in the dormitories, I was back out under the cover of darkness, wreaking my havoc on the 'Clowns'. I decided that on this occasion, I needed to be well away from the cause of disruption so no amount of blame could be laid at my door. I simply placed an aerosol can on their dwindling campfire, and swiftly made my way back to our tent.

What seemed like an eternity passed by, and just when I was dropping off to sleep, an almighty explosion erupted outside bringing the entire camp to its feet. In the ensuing chaos that was generated by the eruption, the fire brigade were called. All the scouts were removed from the near vicinity, and asked to gather at the fire assembly point next to the main entrance. Questions were asked, bollockings given, tears shed, and voices raised, in fact the works. During the entire melee, I just stood there, looking downcast and pretending to be tired, by yawning every thirty seconds.

No one bothered to ask me anything about the detonation of the mini time bomb, so I didn't have to tell any lies, which exonerated me from the blame. Well it did in my mind. All the scouts were eventually comforted and reassured about their safety. The aerosol can had taken flight, and landed in the nearby chapel, smashing the stained glass window. There would be hell to pay in the morning, and it was rumoured that the police had been informed and would be attending the site the next morning, to question all the competitors and get to the bottom of the bomb maker.

As I was wearily making my way down to the dormitory, the Chief Scout came rushing out into the cold night air, all flustered and embarrassed, with the 'Brown Owl' behind him, pulling her dressing gown down. I heard him say to one of the leaders,

"What the fuck was that?"

I chuckled to myself thinking, that the Mayor of Hiroshima probably used the very same words when the Americans dropped the atom bomb.

The following morning all the delegates were lined up for Morning Prayers and raising the flag. I'd thought of hoisting up Brown Owl's panties when I spotted them hanging on the clothes line that previous evening, but good sense got the better of me. I was glad that the idea of stealing knickers had escaped my mind, and that I'd just concentrated my efforts on causing chaos in the tents. The police didn't turn up, so the telling off was somewhat subdued; even in the '70s the police often couldn't be bothered to attend insignificant events, like explosions and arson.

In a decade of rampant inflation when prices soared leading to high unemployment, the cops concentrated their efforts on policing strikes caused by unhappy trade union members. In their confrontations with the unions, they could happily beat the shit out of them with their truncheons and get away scot-free. They'd been granted an unofficial license by the government to hit people willy-nilly that stood up for what they believed in. The added bonus for the coppers was that they could also reel in hundreds of pounds in overtime money. It was a win-win situation for them. This, coupled with the troubles in Northern Ireland, kept our bobbies relatively busy and off the streets at the time.

I didn't care whether or not the police turned up; as far as I was concerned, this was a matter for scouts and scouts only. It was neither fish nor fowl, in my book. The night's events were soon forgotten and the competition was soon back in full swing. We won the first three events, these being rope bridge building, knots and lashings, and knife and axe techniques. Saturday afternoon brought canoeing activities on the pond. I loved canoeing, from the first time I sat in the cockpit of an orange fibreglass kayak on the River Wye in Herefordshire.

The modern kayak is derived from the Inuit (Arctic Eskimo) model, with a keel. The single-seater I used had an upturned bow for better performance on the water. Once comfortably sat in a kayak, with the spray-deck, (a flexible material which fastens snugly around the waist and edges of the cockpit, to cover the opening), fastened onto the lip of the cockpit, one is secure in the knowledge that both legs and camping gear remain dry.

Our specific tasks that particular day were to carry out a series of manoeuvres on the water, both forwards and backwards through a slalomed course, do an 'Eskimo roll' whilst remaining inside the kayak, and to capsize in a proper and controlled manner. Piece of piss, I thought, this baby was mine. The guys duly elected me to represent them. I was last on the water, and watching the previous shower of shits from other troops, I knew I had nothing to worry about. My manoeuvrability in the canoe was second to none, so the first part of the exercise went to plan. A full Eskimo roll can be difficult, but once again I pulled this off with ease. It was at this stage of the competition that I'd realised that I'd won. For my finale, all I had to do was capsize; this is what all novice canoeists are taught within the first hour of attempting the sport. *Crikey Moses,* with fifty or so onlookers, as well as the judges, I thought I'd spice things up a bit.

Rocking my canoe gently on the pond, I pretended to become possessed, and started going berserk. With arms flailing and intermittent screams, I flipped my kayak over. Whilst the canoe was upside down, I slipped out of the cockpit, and up righted myself under the water but with my head inside the upturned canoe. The cockpit acted as an air pocket, so I stayed there inside the kayak, treading water with my feet, making the spectators think I was drowning. Through the fibreglass sides of the vessel I could clearly hear raised voices concerned about my safety.

After several seconds, the people on the bank side started hollering my name in vain. I remained calm and steadfast in my underwater tomb. There was no way I was going to make my way to the surface, until at least three of the instructors had dived into the dark waters to rescue me. At last I heard loud splashes, and fathomed my instructors were on the way to my aid. Just when two of them rammed into the canoe, I surfaced, wearing a smug look on my face. My comrades cheered with delight—unlike my rescuers. Thus I was disqualified from the event, for putting my life and the lives of my instructors at risk. All I can say on the matter in hindsight is some people have no sense of humour…

Saturday night was somewhat of a let-down after the frivolity of the previous night's revelries and the fun I'd had on the pond that afternoon. I was feeling tired and fatigued, but I didn't dare go to sleep due to the fear of one of my fellow camp mates playing tricks on me. Larry suggested that we take part in a few games he'd played when attending the main Jamboree earlier that year. Everyone agreed in principle, and he began to explain the first contest. You have to take into account I was only fourteen years old at the time. Even though, like most teenagers I thought I knew everything, Larry's games opened my eyes up to a different world; a world I didn't want to participate in.

The first game was called 'Soggy Biscuit'. He placed a digestive biscuit on the ground, and suggested that we all took our cocks out and pleasured ourselves over the biscuit. The last one to ejaculate onto the unsuspecting crumbs had to eat it, gentlemen's relish and all. What kind of game was this I asked myself? Surprisingly no one other than Larry wanted to try this event, so Larry wacked off on the biscuit there and then and subsequently ate it. I was gobsmacked at what I had just witnessed.

The next game he suggested was just as bizarre. He called it the 'Fireman's Hose' which involved us all lying in a line next to each other, and placing our hands on the erect penises of the boys to our immediate right and left. On his command, it was pump away. At this I immediately exited the tent and confessed all my wrongdoings to the Chief Scout. I felt that I'd be safer inside a police cell than with Larry the *fudge-packer*.

Chapter 5
De La Salle

Attending an all boys' school is something of a culture shock; being taught by monks takes it to a whole new level. The first years at Beauchief Hall were strange for me. I didn't fit in with the majority of other kids, and certainly felt shunned or left out somewhat by the teachers. Beauchief itself is a beautiful, affluent area of Sheffield, and Beauchief Hall sat in its own splendid grounds, surrounded by mature trees, ornamental ponds, and fantastic playing fields. In the third year, pupils were moved to Scott Road in the Pitsmoor district of the city (pits by name and pits by nature). Things that stick out in my mind from this period of my life include exam pressure, puberty, muggings, and magpies—there were hundreds of the robbing buggers. Magpies are known as the pirates of the skies.

Pitsmoor was an area of outstanding natural violence. Muggings became a popular pastime with its residents. Whilst waiting for the bus we would regularly get stopped and asked for money, even if we were in a gang of say ten, and the mugger was by himself. Safety in numbers didn't come into it with these bandits. Whenever we got stopped, the mugger in question always asked for the same amount of money; two pence. If you're going to rob someone, I'd have gone for a lot more than two pence, considering the consequences of getting caught, but this small amount took you everywhere by South Yorkshire Transport in those days. One afternoon, I left school early for a hospital appointment. My teacher or guardian failed to show, so I tootled off myself. Northern General Hospital was only a few miles away, so I decided to walk, well run if the truth be known.

I arrived unscathed and within twenty minutes was bandaged accordingly and sent on my merry way back to class. Checking that the coast was clear, I set off like the wind, my shoes burning rubber on the tarmac causeways. I was fit back then, and had the physique of a racing snake. In no time at all, I could see the steps leading up to the main gates. A false sense of security set in, and I slowed down for the last few hundred yards; big mistake. From behind the wall, two West Indian youths jumped out and accosted me. They requested the obligatory two-pence, which I immediately began to rummage around in my pants for. Shit, I thought, I'm bloody *pink lint*. Just my luck, normally even I would have had two-pence. I began to fret somewhat and dig ever deeper into my pants, frantically searching for a few coppers.

Whenever I get into situations like these, I get aroused down below for no apparent reason. Please don't ask me why, I know it sounds perverted and pathetic. No matter to what depth my hand ventured, no cash was forthcoming, and from my assailant's perspective, it must have looked like I was playing pocket snooker. One of them looked at me perplexed and said,

"How long are you going to be *jacking off* man? The bus is here. We need to be in town by half two. Just give us the *dosh* or we'll cut your dick off."

"There's more chance of finding my dick down there than a two pence piece," I replied.

At this the two guys scurried off to catch the bus, and I legged it back to school. Luck was on my side that day.

During the majority of lessons, I would sit staring aimlessly out of the window, wishing my life away. The teachers were very strict in those days, and failing to pay attention could lead to getting a severe reprimand in front of the entire class, or worse still being sent to the Headmaster's Office. Being situated at the rear of the classroom adjacent the window gave me some leverage on this score. I did get sent to see the Head, but usually for something far more creative than being inattentive.

On one occasion I recall being in a physics lesson, discussing weight ratios. A group of us were tasked to set up a system of levers and pulleys to test out some bloody theory or another. The physics lab had a very high ceiling, with a metal lattice strung underneath with fixed pulley wheels at intervals. We threaded our allotted rope through one of the pulley wheels and carefully created a harness, which was then duly wrapped around one of our colleagues, namely Hardy. With everything in place, we set about our experiment of hauling Hardy up to the ceiling, demonstrating the theory behind effort versus load. Just as we were about to begin, our teacher Selwyn Meatball was summoned to the staff room.

With all supervision gone out of the door, playtime commenced. Several of us tied Hardy up with the remainder or the rope so he was trussed like a Christmas turkey. With brute strength we yanked him upwards so fast that he smashed his head on the solid bars strewn across the ceiling. Following the almighty crack of cranium against solid object, his head flopped down; basically he was out for the count. This joyous scientific act caused huge excitement with all our classmates; cheers rang out around the laboratory. Individuals, armed with elastic bands and paper pellets, proceeded to use Hardy as target practise. Pellets were assaulting him right, left and centre, and all the lads got involved, such was Hardy's popularity with his fellow classmates.

After the onslaught of paper missiles, Jafe, the tallest lad in the school, connected a long orange rubber hose up to a gas tap that was situated underneath our victim. Potter turned the gas on, and Jafe duly ignited the end of the pipe, creating a mini flame-thrower. As Jafe was so tall, he managed to point the flame directly under Hardy's rear, and *hey presto,* Hardy was awoken from his forced sleep. Further merriment ensued from the assembled group of sadists. Youths can be right bastards sometimes. Our version of 'Hannibal Lecter' was now fuming, and demanding to be let down. Not on your nelly, we thought. Hardy also happened to be afraid of heights; this just got better. Jafe then took it on himself to start to burn the bottom of the rope which was holding Hardy aloft. More screams of joy from the baying group. Then it all went pear-shaped. Selwyn entered the room, accompanied by Strapper Simmons, who terrorised the entire school.

Inevitably the shit hit the fan, and we all got covered in it. Full detentions were handed out, and Jafe and I were summoned to Strapper's office for a little chat, which consisted of him berating us, followed by six lashes of his special leather hand strap across the arse. To cap it all, we were both made to write letters to all involved, these being Hardy, Selwyn and Strapper himself, apologising for our behaviour and misconduct, and wasting Strapper's valuable time. Let me tell you here and now, when Strapper was called into action, he couldn't hide the happiness on his fizzog, such was his thirst for physically chastising young delinquent boys. He chuffing loved it, and might I add, it hurt like hell. Gracious, if boys were beaten in this fashion now there would be a public outcry. The teacher would be sentenced to the salt mines of Siberia, or alternatively forced to join the Conservative party.

The lesson I learned from this unfortunate incident, was that levers, like Strapper's arm, rely on mechanical advantage. The higher the mechanical advantage, the easier to lift the weight, which in Strapper's case was his leather strap. (Mechanical advantage is defined as the ratio of load to effort.) He needed very little effort or persuasion in dishing out his corporal punishment on my backside. Pulley systems rely on this same relationship. The load bearing of the strap connecting with my arse was completely disproportionate to the effort Strapper put into the thrashing. So there you have it, physics made simple. This teaching lark is easy.

Sticking to the sciences, another subject I detested was chemistry. I was unfortunate enough to have the same teacher throughout my entire secondary education at De La Salle. He was from Burnley, which speaks volumes. The man was a bully, a drunk, a half-wit and a nob-cheese. I loathed the guy with all my heart. He delighted in belittling me in front of the rest of the class for my accent and ignorance of chemistry. Looking back over these wasted lessons, I now realise that he wasn't cut out to be a teacher at all. He frequently admitted he despised being around kids, which is somewhat strange when you are employed as a tutor.

Chemistry is a subject that never caught my imagination; periodic tables, atomic structures, acids and alkalis. Knowing the chemical symbol for copper is of no use if you want to iron your shirt, have sex with an older woman, or indeed connect your testicles to the car's jump-leads for kicks. I ask you, who gets off on this kind of crap? The answer is chemists and potential bomb-makers.

During one particular lesson, our chemistry teacher Mr. Beech had to leave the classroom, in order that he could quench his secret thirst for alcohol in the staff toilets. Whilst he was absent, a few of us decided to hold an impromptu farting competition with a difference; we intended to ignite the farts with lighted Bunsen burners. Being a Maltby lad, I've always been able to fart at will, such was my classy upbringing. Several lads started a little betting syndicate, and all the smart money was on me. My competition was a lad named Mac. He was alright, but not in my league when it came to breaking wind.

I squatted on top of the large wooden desk that ran the length of the room, legs akimbo astride the ignited burner. With a little waddle, I was ready to fire. I acknowledged my audience, then let rip, causing a blue flame to rise upwards, setting my Bri-Nylon shirt afire. At that precise moment, old Beech staggered in, and was greeted by me, minus a fringe, and a large gaping hole on my chest where my shirt once lived. He went ape-shit, smacking me straight across the face with the palm of his hand, knocking me to the floor. I kid you not, such was his brutality, it rendered me semi-conscious. As the old adage goes, "Laughter turns to crying," and following his hefty blow, I was now on the verge of blubbing.

Not a sorry or *kiss your arse* did I receive from Beech. He loved doling out his correction at every opportunity. I'm not suggesting for an instant that I shouldn't have received a bollocking, but a whack in the temple isn't big or clever. I managed to clamber up with the support of my mates, and the lesson carried on as if nothing had happened.

When I finally left De La Salle in the summer of 1977, I bumped into Beech on the main corridor leading to the chemistry lab. By now I had grown somewhat, and was starting to fill out. Bullies hate being confronted, so here was my chance to redress the balance. He saw me walking towards him, and realising my intentions, started screaming and hollering in pain, as if I was hitting him. He was acting like a man gone mad, head down, arms flailing around, kicking out at fresh air.

Such a rumpus attracted quite a gathering of spectators, including Strapper Simmons. The fact that I was nowhere near him, made the situation look all the more surreal. Simmons looked straight into my eyes, but this time faced up to the fact that I was about to leave school for good, and I didn't care anymore. There was no way on earth that either he or Beech would get the better of me on this occasion.

Strapper lunged forward, but this time towards Beech, grabbing him by the collar of his jacket, and hurling him into the side of the corridor wall. He then assumed a protective human shield in front of Beech, presuming I was going to hit him. He presumed right, because had Strapper not been there to protect him, I'd have leathered that bastard big time. I've come to hate bullies over the years, and always made it my business to stand up to them at every opportunity. Nine out of ten times, bullies back down. They hate and fear confrontation, and tend to turn tail and scarper.

I once confronted a bully whilst holidaying in 'Tener-fucking-rife,' as it is now affectionately referred to. Me and my family were having dinner one evening in a local restaurant by the seashore. Two tables removed from me sat a big guy from Pontefract, all mouth and braces. He was one of those chaps who could tell you the price of everything, but knew the value of nothing. He was also extremely loud and obnoxious, belittling his wife, and scaring his three young children. During the day, he had obviously consumed quite a lot of 'senorita-beater lager' and the effects were beginning to kick in. He abused the waiters, complained to the owner, and ridiculed his fellow diners. He was a complete and utter tosser.

After ten minutes or so, I had finally had enough of this tyrant, and against my wife's better judgement, decided to confront him face-to-face. As I sauntered over towards him, he was still spouting off, about suing the restaurant and closing it down because it wasn't up to his expectations. He was oblivious to the upset he was causing all the other guests, who were now beginning to feel threatened and intimidated. Having reached his table, I tapped him on the shoulder and asked him to calm down a little. He was now in full swing, barking orders and threats to his kids; this really pissed me off. I then proceeded to grab him by his shirt collar, and yanked his head around to face me. The guy was shell-shocked, and jumped to his feet. The one thing I hadn't managed to factor into my plans was just how big he really was.

"What the frigging hell do you think you're doing Baldy?" he yelled into my face.

Ignoring the gravity of my actions, and not really knowing what the consequences were going to be, I was somewhat upset at his use of the word 'Baldy'. Challenging me was one thing, challenging my dearth of hair follicles was another. Now he was really starting to get my dander up.

"Have you heard the expression, one in the eye is better than three in the ear."

"What the hell are you talking about you numpty?" he replied.

At that, I shoved my index finger straight into his left eye socket, all the way up to my knuckle.

"That's what I mean, you loud-mouthed arse-hole. Keep it down or I'll black both your eyes," I said, all masterful.

The guy winced in pain and was now bent over double. My actions gave me Titanic delight, and for a few seconds, calm was restored. The thing that most surprised me was the way his wife and kids jumped to his defence and started to try to help him. Jesus I thought, only two minutes earlier he had been bullying the lot of them. The guy uprighted himself, and stormed off in the direction of another bar. All my fellow diners burst into a spontaneous round of applause; I felt like a gladiator. That was until his wife slipped her stiletto shoe off, and brained me across the head, knocking me out cold. The lesson here is, don't stick your nose into a bully's business, without first checking his wife's footwear.

Chapter 6
Coleman's Youth Club

Entertainment for bored youths was pretty basic back in the '70s. When the Coleman Youth Centre opened its doors for the first time, Maltby night life soared. The 'Yuffie' was open for business for the kids on Thursday and Sunday nights and it rocked to the sound of the Rubettes and Billy Ocean. 'Sugar Baby Love' and 'Juke Box Jive' belted out through the doors, over the adjacent market stalls, and teenagers started to dance and get pregnant.

The centre was quite small and multi-functional; activities included scout meetings, jumble sales, coffee morning and shagging in the toilets when Father Sultan wasn't watching. It was named after Father Coleman who was the late local parish priest. It was predominantly Catholics who attended, mixed with a few Protestants who had been barred from the main youth club annexed to Maltby Comprehensive School. Here Catholics felt relatively safe and would congregate en masse to slag off and plot against the Protestants; the same Protestants that they lived next door to and played in the same football teams with.

Thursdays were okay, but it was Sunday nights that really hit the sweet spot for me; hating school as I did, the club offered me sanctuary and happiness for a few hours on an evening. The thing that floated my particular boat was that it was dark and full of *crumpet*. These girls were gagging for it, as far as I was concerned. Getting off with some of the rampant nymphomaniacs was easy; they also sought refuge here away from their domineering parents, and felt the need to be sexually stimulated, both physically and mentally. Due to the strict Catholic upbringing most of us had to endure and the constant indoctrination of hypocritical bullshit thrust down our throats, when we arrived at the club it was as if we were having a free-for-all, a haven for letting your hair down. Believe you me, we did!

No sooner had the music started pumping and the lights dimmed down we were at it like rabbits; the main sport for the lads was 'fingering' and 'titting-up'. However sordid and immoral this may sound to you, we all did it. The lads were clumsy, ham-fisted and desperate to make contact with the female form, any way they could. The lack of sexual education in Catholic schools, coupled with rigid parental rules meant that at the first opportunity a boy or a girl could experiment and go over to the 'dark side,' they did. Very little intercourse took place within the confines of the 'Yuffie'; that all happened in the empty market stalls outside, away from the vigilant and prying eyes of the youth workers.

One specific evening that springs to mind was when Smig and I had arranged to meet up with a couple of girls down the Crags, to get to know them better and see their faces before it got dark. When Smig turned up I was amazed to see both his arms plastered and bandaged; he resembled a carpet fitter carrying two big rolls under each arm.

He had fallen off his horse that morning and had been rushed to hospital for treatment. He did look a bit of a dip-stick with both his arms in plaster, but when his current girlfriend turned up she became all 'Florence Nightingale' over him, as only girls do. He played to the audience like only a skilful, lying hypochondriac would, and milked the situation for all that it was worth. My girl also started to feel sorry for him, but I soon put that right by telling her that he'd got a dose of the clap. She went nowhere near him after that.

Having arrived at the club we made our way into one of the murky, dirty corners of the room to indulge in our crimes of passion with our respective partners. As the words from 'Red Light Spells Danger' resounded off the walls, we totally ignored the lyrical advice and began fondling and fumbling as only young inexperienced adolescents do. After thirty minutes of 'sucking face' I came up for air and decided to go and wash my hands. Smig followed me into the toilets, looking somewhat bemused.

"What's the matter mate?" I asked.

"Something's not quite right. When I was squeezing her boob it felt rock hard and knobbly, not squidgy like normal. I can't fathom it out. And she kept fidgeting," he replied.

I looked at him with equal bewilderment, mirroring his expression. Shaking my head I made my way to the sweet counter to purchase a bottle of Tab Coke. Standing in the queue directly in front of me was Smig's beloved talking to another girl. I distinctly heard her say that Smig had been caressing her elbow for twenty minutes, and what kind of pervert does that? I looked over to where Smig was sitting and gestured to him quietly that he was a nob-head. Having eventually explained what the girl had said, Smig flushed and became quite upset. He glanced up and saw his girlfriend leaving; she didn't even say goodbye. I nudged Smig and said,

"I think she's given you the elbow buddy."

Of course, teenagers have always been badly behaved. That is the prerogative of youth. There's always been a disconnection between young and old, and so there should be; it is how big the gap is that really matters. I recently read a report stating that Britain faces a crisis in relations between the generations. Back in my day teenagers did exactly what today's teenagers do now, only without the use of drugs, knives and guns; we still had lots of sex, we still smoked, we still drank alcohol and we got into fights. We did, however, show more respect to our elders, and we were allowed to interact more with grown-ups without the consternation of being interfered with, or them being classed as paedophiles.

There are many reasons for the estrangement between kids and adults, and the main cause of this is the mistrust directed at adults. I blame it on the obsessive protective parenting culture which most of us subscribe to. British attitudes towards child-adult encounters are tainted with suspicion; no longer can a parent interact with a child who doesn't belong to them. Adults now feel awkward and even anxious when they are in the company of groups of kids. I've witnessed numerous occasions where adults have taken themselves out of situations deemed to be dodgy. The death of 'common sense' has lot to do with this. Adults are terrified of being stigmatised, classed as being a pervert or 'kiddie-feeler'. If all kids are taught to mistrust all adults and treat them as potential child molesters, it becomes very difficult for adults to interact and socialise with young people on a personal level.

Our youth leaders were able to interact with us on a very personal level; they hit us, supplied us with cheap booze, and some of the older ones slept with us on a regular basis. It never affected me or did me any harm, apart from leaving me permanently walking bow-legged, and having a profound desire to dress up as Gary Glitter.

Getting back to the youth club, one evening a lad called Peter turned up paralytic after consuming vast quantities of cider. He was staggering all over the shop, bumping into people and generally being obnoxious. On noticing his unacceptable behaviour Father Sultan escorted him off the premises, as only he could. He hit him so hard in the belly that Peter crashed through the main entrance doors and hit the perimeter dwarf wall some six feet away. To compound matters, when he connected with the wall, he emptied the entire contents of his stomach over a courting couple, who happened to be sat on the wall in the throes of serious *snogging*. The projectile vomit came out like Linda Blair's 'The Exorcist,' and covered the unfortunate lovers from head to toe. It was dark at the time, and the area surrounding the club was deserted, apart from me and the sick-splattered sweethearts.

Peter collapsed to the ground, as Father Sultan slammed the doors shut. I was left in total shock at what I'd just seen. The couple fled the scene, with the woman screaming hysterically and the bloke cursing. Being a decent sort of lad, I ignored Peter's plea for help, and tootled off to the chippy, as I was craving a battered onion ring. Later that same evening on my way home on the bus, I happened to be sat behind a lady whose 'Bee-hive' hair style was adorned with bits of peas and carrots. As I got off the bus I felt compelled to check out her identity. To my utter astonishment and delight, I suddenly realised it was my cousin Chesswood, cross-dressing again. He was wearing a wig and hadn't become aware of the apparent leftovers still entwined in his tresses. I remember thinking, food for thought...

As I have mentioned on numerous occasions, my formative years growing up in Maltby gave me an insight into real poverty and racism, which can have an isolating effect in a tight-knit Catholic community. Having little money and even less prospects, anyone who turned up at the 'Yuffie' with new clothes was instantly envied and despised in equal measure. I remember one lad arriving attired in Levi stay-press trousers, loafer ox-blood shoes, Ben Sherman black and white checked shirt, and had the audacity to be from a local Protestant family. When he made his grand entrance into the club he was overwhelmed with young fanny because of his attire and demeanour. Me and the other lads instantly loathed him with a passion, the rich *proddie* fucker. My initial reaction was to murder him, but then I realised he was my cousin.

What was I to do? The speakers were blaring out 'Glam Rock' as the voices of Sweet and Alvin Stardust filled the room. Hearing this incited me even more to take action. When my cousin Sal hit the dance floor, my anger reached boiling point as he started to dance like a professional; twisting, turning, pirouetting and the likes. It was bad enough him being dressed like a tart, but being able to strut his funky stuff like a good-un was too much to take in one go. I picked up a glass ash-tray from the coffee table that I was sat at, and hurled it in his direction. Just at the precise moment of impact, the lucky bastard bent down to buff his shoes with his handkerchief, initialled of course.

As luck would have it Father Sultan happened to be stood directly behind him, and unfortunately the glass receptacle hit him straight in the bollocks, much to his dismay. I left the club quicker than a rat runs up a sewer, and never returned again. Father Sultan resembled Bryan Ferry, and was hellishly good looking and as hard as nails. Just because he was a priest didn't mean that he wouldn't dish out a beating. I'd previously seen him leather my mate Peter, so hanging around to deliberate my actions seemed futile. The quicker I got out of there the better. I flew through the doors like a bullet, terrified of him catching me. My penance that night would have been more than a few 'Hail Marys'. The youth club was a place where I felt relatively safe and comfortable. Watching him fall to the floor on his knees, bowing his head in pain, made me think of the church and praying for forgiveness; I was desperate for his forgiveness but I didn't have the bollocks to wait and ask for it, and come to that, neither did he that night.

Chapter 7
Maltby Comp

Having left De La Salle with five olives (O Levels) and four ASBOs (aggressive, stupid, belligerent, outcast), I tried my luck at Maltby Comprehensive, which was on my door step. I should have gone there in the first place, instead of travelling all the way to Sheffield for five years. De La Salle College was supposed to be for the elite boys of South Yorkshire. Who were they trying to kid. I'm sure the extensive travelling messed up my education—along with my lack of intellect, and my gross stupidity.

I was now coming up to seventeen, and the sixth form was something to look forward to. For the first time in ages I would be sat in classrooms full of girls. This was another culture shock, but one I came to relish. Jayne Junior from St. Mary's was to be reunited with me in geography and geology 'A' levels. The two Angelas from the youth club would be there, along with a host of other beauties. Life was beginning to look up, or so I thought.

Maltby Comprehensive was a sprawling school, with little character and even less interest in the little characters who attended it. Some of the teachers were okay like Cherry Foster, Pete Wagland and Mossy. The rest didn't give a shit. On the plus side, I now had settled into a routine with a gang of mates from Cliff Hills. Five of us had decided to stay on in the sixth form to waste a few more valuable years before we had to get a proper job. For the first time in years I felt a certain sense of happiness and belonging. Oh, I was still poor, a virgin, insomniac, manic, but on the whole quite content with what life was throwing at me. The thing that really floated my boat was being in a teenage gang. We didn't need to throw expensive trainers over a telegraph wire to alert you to the fact that you'd entered our turf. We'd just beat the shit out of you for trespassing. It was the law of the jungle. Maltby kids could come and go as they pleased; outsiders weren't welcome. Street fighting started to become the norm, and like rutting stags, if we hadn't anyone to fight with, we'd start a brawl with our mates.

School life was a lot easier for me; I could stay in bed longer, walk to school in fifteen minutes, and there were a lot of free periods. Whenever you didn't have to attend lessons, the idea was to go to the library and study. Bullshit to that for a game of soldiers. We had a common room where me and the lads could show off and pretend we were big hitters. Nearly all the kids who had stayed on at school were bright, intelligent, hard working and conscientious; not us though. Apart from Smig, we were there for the laugh and an easy ride, much to our parents' annoyance.

Personally, I never took this part of my education seriously, as it affected my other primary function at school; messing about. Showing off took up all my time, so there was very little left in the tank for studying. I suddenly realised that challenging authority and being a rebel impressed my peers, and in December 1977, changed my personality over night. No longer would I stress over exams. No more would I attend church. I was free to pretty much do as I pleased. This phase lasted eight minutes; then I was suspended from school.

One evening, the film club were showing a Dracula movie in the main hall. Me and a few of the boys attended out of boredom, or so we would have had you believe. During the interval, I was mistaken for one of my mates, and a fight erupted between me and another sixth-former. Things got a little nasty, and the boy in question took a swift right hook to his jaw, which to this day I am still not proud of. Our Head of Year happened to be at the same movie and involved the police. My adversary at the time dropped all charges, due to the fact he mistook me for someone else. The school, however, decided in their infinite wisdom to press their own charges, and I was fined £70, and got a criminal record for 'Actual Bodily Harm'. For good measure, I was also suspended from school for two weeks. The only other police record I ever got was 'Walking on the Moon'.

The criminal record didn't bother me, neither did the suspension. The fine, however, choked me as I only earned £9 per week on my pools round. How was I going to pay? Fortunately, the magistrate presiding over the proceedings took pity on me, and allowed me to pay it off over thirty weeks at £3 per week, which helped me enormously. In hindsight, I should have just walked away, but my temper got the better of me. The only winner on that occasion was the courts.

After a fortnight of wandering the streets during the day, I was allowed back in school. I decided that things would be different now, and I would turn the other cheek when confronted. This only lasted a few minutes, as when I entered the school gates, some oiks shouted a few obscenities in my direction, and it all kicked off again, with me in the middle of it. Smig intervened and dragged me away, just before the Head of Year appeared. I brushed myself down, and made my way to assembly, which was held every morning in the adjoining youth club. When assembly was over, our illustrious leader read out the roll call of dishonour—which always consisted of me, Chalky, Scone and Russ. On this particular morning, not forgetting I'd been absent from school for the past fortnight, my name wasn't mentioned. The entire congregation looked on in disbelief, me included. As I started to walk away, my name echoed around the round.

"Hart, see me in my office straight after assembly," said the Head.

What the hell have I done now I thought? I've not been here to cause any trouble. He must be mistaken. When I arrived at his office, the callous swine kept me waiting twenty minutes, to make me feel even more anxious and stressed. I knew that if I received another *strike*, I'd be out. Finally I was summoned in; the charge was wearing a flat cap in school hours. I protested my case, stating that in actuality I hadn't been at school for the past fourteen days. The Head said that this was merely a technicality, and I'd been seen by another member of staff, wearing my head gear at a jaunty angle, so the punishment would fit the crime. What crime? Wearing a flat cap in a built up area, how ridiculous was that? Can you imagine this happening in today's society? I accepted the punishment, and walked away crestfallen, knowing my new image of being a rebel was in tatters.

The following week, against all the odds, I was elected a school governor to represent the new intake of pupils into the sixth form. This involved attending a pompous ceremony, and having to wear a crimson cloak. I looked a right prick in this Dickensian apparel, but it really pissed off my enemy the Head of Year. He was mortified that I'd been chosen, and did all in his power to stop it, but to no avail. Part of my duties was to attend the Christmas Concert with the real governors who presided over the welfare of the school.

The Chair of the governors was the late Lord Scarborough, and I was asked to meet and greet him in the staff room, and be his escort for the day. Lord Scarborough was the only nobility I was ever likely to meet, so I was ecstatic to be his lap dog. When poor people meet the landed gentry, they seldom know how to act or speak, for fear of embarrassing themselves. Lord Scarborough put me straight at ease by offering me several glasses of sherry to conquer my inhibitions, and by George it did the trick. I instantly became his bat-man, and you would have thought me and his Lordship were a double act. He was marvellous, and slowly throughout the day I got sloshed to the point that I couldn't speak, which was a blessing for the rest of the attendees. The Head of Year noticed my inebriated demeanour, and pulled me to one side.

"Hart, stick to water. Water is the matrix of life," he said, looking down his nose at me.

"And sherry is the origin of death," was my garbled reply.

Why I responded in this way was anyone's guess, but the vast quantities of alcohol I'd consumed certainly played a large part in it. Following the concert, I began to develop a taste for booze, along with the rest of my pals. We started to frequent the White Swan public house, and the Manor Hotel, both in Maltby. The Swan was the pub to be seen in; it had a reputation that spread for miles. I once had the great pleasure of meeting Peter Stringfellow in his London night club, and when I mentioned where I was from, he immediately acknowledged the White Swan, and said what an excellent venue it used to be. On a weekend you couldn't get in due to its popularity, but during the weekday afternoon sessions it was accessible. Mind you, we did have to hide our school blazers and ties so we didn't look so conspicuous. Money was always tight, so we could only afford the odd pint of beer or lager. To make it last and have the desired effect, we used to drink it through a straw. What a set of *wallies* we must have looked to the other customers.

Going back into school after consuming a few pints isn't recommended practice. Getting caught consuming bitter in the pub by your Head of Year is just as bad. On one afternoon session, several of us had decided to go and play snooker at the Manor Hotel; the alternative was an economics class. We divested our blazers and ties outside, stashed them in the corner of the vestibule to the public bar, and marched in all cocky and full of attitude. Waltzing up to the bar I asked the landlord for two pints of bitter. He looked at me rather strangely and asked if I was eighteen. I was somewhat puzzled, as we'd being going into this particular pub every day for the past two weeks. The barman's enunciation was noticeably peculiar, placing unwarranted emphasis on the word "eighteen". Out of the corner of my eye, lurking in the smoke-filled room, lying in wait for us was our Head. Following a pregnant pause, I looked straight into the landlord's eyes and said,

"Do you take it up to the shitter?"

Now both the publican and our Head of Year appeared astounded at my question, and stood there gobsmacked.

"Well do you?" I persisted.

After this second remark I was barred from the premises on the spot. I accepted his invitation to leave, collected my belongings and returned to economics class, somewhat late, but content with my quick thinking. Being able to think on my feet has saved me from many a scrape in my time. A few years ago, my wife, brother and sister-in-law went to Sheffield for a night out. On arriving in the city centre, our kid and his missus decided to go for an Indian meal, leaving my wife and me to wait for them in a nearby pub. The bar we visited was packed, and my first inclination was to go elsewhere, but my 'trouble and strife' decided we'd stay.

Whilst I was getting served, a group of Australian Neanderthal rugby players came in and stood directly behind me waiting their turn. One gargantuan chap was virtually resting on my shoulders such was his proximity to me, and I by the smell of his breathe, he'd obviously had a few *sherbets* earlier that day. By complete accident, I stepped backwards, and placed my entire weight on his foot, crushing his toes in the process. I pretended nothing had happened and began to collect my drinks from the barmaid. Looking into the back fitting mirror, I could see the guy writhing in pain, and all his comrades were fussing over him, trying to ascertain why he was hurting so much. Within seconds, the injured party tapped me on the shoulder. He had the look of a wounded lion written over his face and I could sense that I was in for a pounding. I completely ignored him again, which seemed to rile him even further. He then grabbed me by the throat, and his chimps surrounded me.

"You've just stamped on my foot you pommie bastard, and haven't had the decency to apologise. I think I'm going to have to teach you a lesson in good manners," he bellowed in my face.

I looked straight at him, then turned to his minders, and started to mimic sign language as used by deaf and dumb people. I know what you're thinking, what kind of shallow, wet lettuce would do such a thing? The answer was me! Even though I was totally outnumbered. It was an unfortunate accident, and most importantly, I'd just had my teeth done at the orthodontist at a cost of two grand that very morning, and I didn't want to part with them so quickly. I'm sure the deaf and dumb population will forgive me for my mockery of their mode of communication, but it certainly helped me that night. Better still, the rugby player insisted on buying our drinks for us as a way of apologising to me. The lesson here is, think on your feet, not someone else's.

I didn't make it to the end of the lower sixth before I was expelled. I always told everyone I was suspended again, but now the truth's out. The Head of Year finally gathered enough shit on me that I had no choice; jump or be pushed. I will never forget the look of delirium on his face when he escorted me out through the main gates. His parting words to me were,

"Hart, you will make nothing of your life. You are a waster, a clown, a lout and an oik."

I took great umbrage to the word "oik", only because at the time I didn't know that it meant an obnoxious or unpleasant person.

Chapter 8
Knock-Out Don

On leaving school, I had the good fortune of meeting a lad who went by the name of 'Knock-out Don'. He earned this magnificent title because of his boxing prowess. Don had boxed in twenty amateur fights, and was knocked out in all of them in the first round. It's some feat when you come to think of it. The ironic thing about 'Knock-out' was that on the streets, he was as hard as nails, and handy with the *dukes*. No one would come near him, and no one ever offered him out for fear of a good beating. I saw him in action on numerous occasions up against as many as five other lads, and he always came out on top. Don was a far better street fighter than a boxer.

Like me, Don came from a poor family. The big difference between Don and I was that he was always happy. He had a smile from ear to ear, and would make people laugh at the drop of a hat, such was his sense of humour. He was a kid who could laugh at his own misfortune; if, however, you laughed at it, he would leather you. He wasn't a big lad by any stretch of the imagination, but he was as solid as a brick shit-house.

On a lazy Sunday morning I decided to call for Don, to see if he wanted to aimlessly wander the streets, or even play a mindless staring competition, such was my boredom. When I arrived at his house,

I was greeted by Don's beetroot face, spewing up all over his dad's dahlias. Wiping his mush, he turned to me and started to laugh out loud. I was somewhat bewildered by this, but he began to explain to me what he was laughing at.

"Hey Alf, listen to this me old mucker. It'll make you piss your sides," Don said.

He then enlightened me on what was amusing him so much. Apparently, his Uncle Bert had been involved in an incident earlier that morning at the local pit.

Grafting down the mines was and still is a hard, dirty job. Back then, my Grandad would tell me it got so hot working at a depth of 3000 feet, he'd have to strip down to his undies due to the tremendous temperatures, which could reach up to 100 degrees Fahrenheit. He said the miners had to drink vast reservoirs of water from their *dudleys* to replace lost fluids; a miner could lose between 4 to 6lbs in sweat during each working hour, and had to supplement the water with salt tablets.

When Don's uncle Bert had gone to work the night shift that previous evening, he had taken a bottle of *Tizer* with him. Now Tizer wasn't your run-of-the-mill tea, or water; it was a sought after fizzy drink, that cost a bob or two, and Bert loved the stuff with a passion. When break time came around he was horrified to find out that someone had drunk his amber nectar. What thieving swine would carry out such a dastardly deed? Bert's temper was now at boiling point, and reached into his knapsack and pulled out a large claw-hammer.

"What are you going to do with that Bert?" one of his colleagues shouted, looking all quizzical.

"I'm waiting for the first bastard to burp, and then I'm going to kill him," was Bert's reply.

Briefly stopping to catch his breath, Don carried on telling me another mining yarn involving my Uncle Tony. Tony's speciality was playing practical jokes on his workmates. His particular favourite was one where he would skive off, and hide behind a fellow miner who wanted to take a dump. Down in the bowels of the Earth, when a collier needed to shit, he would just tootle off, squat down, and *Bob's your uncle'*, jobbie done there and then. The smelly excrement would then be popped into a bag and disposed of in the proper manner.

Uncle Tony however, decided to change the routine; armed with a shovel would wait in ambush for his intended victim. Tony would act with the expertise of the SAS, never letting the bloke know he was in such close proximity. When the guy dropped his *kecks*, Tony would deftly place the shovel under his arse, and catch the turd in mid-flight. Swiftly the shovel would be retracted, and Tony would melt back into the pitch-black surroundings, like Gollum in Tolkien's 'The Lord of the Rings'. Finishing off his ablutions, the guy would then automatically shine his miner's lamp to see where the *tommy* had been deposited, so he could clear it up. Imagine the disconcerted look on his face, when after scouring the black terrain for half an hour and not finding it, finally concluding that the log must be back from whence it came (inside his underpants).

To add insult to injury, later on during the same shift, Tony would cleverly wrap the crap to make it resemble a lunch pack. With expert timing he'd softly place it on the moving conveyor belt carrying all the clumps of coal out from underground, and quickly telephone the poor sufferer who had previously misplaced his shit, and tell him that he'd inadvertently dropped his sandwiches onto the conveyor, and could he retrieve them for him. Tony would fiendishly add a drop of Tizer to the faeces for extra liquidity and impact. What a complete and utter tormentative bastard my uncle was, but I loved him dearly, and still miss him enormously.

Don, in his infinite wisdom, decided he didn't need to go to school, so he stopped attending when he was thirteen. It was interfering with his other more important pastimes: women and fighting. In later years, Don confided that he'd an aversion to the word 'school,' and this was one of the main reasons for his prolonged absence.

I recently read an article in a local newspaper about a school in Sheffield being referred to as a 'Place for Learning'. The boffins in charge thought the word 'school' had negative connotations. What kind of society are we now living in? These do-gooder politically correct arseholes need to get a reality check and join the rest of the human race; if not, please kindly leave Blighty, and piss off elsewhere....we don't want you!

I recently heard a woman spouting off in our local pub, referring to teachers as 'furnishers of information'. She went on to add that classrooms were 'wisdom acquisition zones', and best of all, detention was now a 'period of reflection'. What utter nonsense. When I got detention, the only thing I reflected on was the impending thrashing I was going to get with the pit-belt when I arrived home. Mind you, the belt made us what we are today...deranged.

Another thing that made Don so different from me was his entrepreneurial nature. He seemed to want to break away from our mutual privation far more than I did. Don realised that life didn't owe him a living; he had to get out there and earn it for himself. When he was ten years old, he used to collect empty bottles from all over the neighbourhood and return them to the shop where they were bought, and get tuppence on each bottle for his trouble.

One morning, Don noticed the shop owner stacking all the empties in his back yard. It was at this juncture in his young life that he decided that it would be far easier to steal the bottles from the shopkeeper's rear yard, and later return them via the front door, as if he'd collected them legally. It was also far easier on the legs and took a fraction of the time. Initially, the shopkeeper was delighted with Don's efforts and rewarded him accordingly. When the penny finally dropped, Don was chased through the streets of Maltby with an axe such was the owner's embarrassment and anger. Don, however, made a tidy sum from his ill-gotten gains, and bought a motor-bike from the proceeds.

Even in the face of adversity, Don showed true mettle and was never *chicken-shit*. Grown-ups didn't frighten him, and neither did the police. His audacity and nerve was second to none. I remember him going into a betting office on the Queens Corner when he was only fifteen years old. Obviously he was well underage to be seen in a gambling establishment, but he still marched in, larger than life, to place a bet for his dad. On seeing Don entering the premises the bookmaker leapt over the counter, grabbed him by his shirt collar, and proceeded to march him back out. Without blinking an eye, Don delivered a beautiful upper cut to the bookmaker's jaw and felled him; he hit the ground like a sack of spuds. Don then calmly placed his bet with the spotty assistant behind the counter, who was now in a state of complete panic, and slowly made his way to the exit. Several onlookers who witnessed the spectacle stood silent in total disbelief. Don coolly acknowledged them by tipping his flat cap, and jokingly said,

"Hey chaps, you ought to have a bet on 'Smelly Fanny' in the next race at Doncaster. It's never been licked."

One day Don suggested that we have a stroll down to the Crags, where I soon found he wanted to discuss women in the most sordid graphic detail. Teenage boys are under tremendous pressure to lie to their peers when it comes to girls. The first question thrown at you when meeting up with a gang of testosterone challenged young men is "Did you get anything?" I often wanted to say:

"Yes indeed I did. I got ridiculed about the size of my manhood. I got laughed at by how quickly I ejaculated. She positively wet herself about my sparse pubic hair. Oh, and yes, she told me she had given me herpes."

I never did manage to say this; I just pretended like all the rest of the guys that the girls said that I was hung like a donkey, as hairy as a chimp, lasted a good five minutes in the act (this is normally how long it takes, isn't it?), and the only herpes I caught was the cold sore on my bottom lip. Young lads are pathetic when it comes to lying. Any girl with an ounce of sense sees straight through this sham with ease, but lads take it all in, believing every word as if it were gospel, such is their gullibility.

Don didn't seem to have a problem attracting girls. They seemed to flock around him like flies round shit. In my humble opinion, girls are captivated by boys who are strong, manly and 'in charge'. Don ticked all these boxes; I ticked none. He could pull a bird without trying, such was his charisma. He would frequently say to me,

"Alf, I bet you a pound to a pinch of shit I'll have her knickers off in ten minutes."

More often than not, he was right. The only time he was wrong with such a boast was when he'd got inebriated on Bull's Blood—red wine, bought from the local off-license. The woman who spurned his advances on this particular occasion was my cousin Chesswood; the only reason he turned Don down was because he was on his period. It would have been wonderful if Chesswood had accepted Don's drunken proposal and consummated the relationship 'Chesswood style'. I remind Don now and again how lucky he was that day and how lightly his bottom got off with just a pounding. Don's retort to me is always the same,

"Don't knock it until you've tried it." Enough said I think!

On arriving at the Crags, the weather started to take a turn for the worse. In the distance, dark, heavy clouds were forming, and rain was imminent. Don turned to me and said,

"It looks black over Elsie's mother's. We better make tracks Alf and find some shelter afore we get piss-wet through."

Hidden at the bottom of the limestone escarpment was a small cave. Not many kids knew of its existence, as the entrance to the cavity was covered with dense foliage. Don scrambled through the undergrowth and made his way into the dry shelter.

"Hurry up Alf. The heavens are about to open," Don beckoned.

At that point, a bolt of lightning struck a tree no more than five feet away from me. The noise and the shock threw me to the ground, and for several seconds I was in stunned into a state of suspended animation. The trunk was split longitudinally from top to bottom, opening up the tree, exposing its very soul. It seemed to scream out in pain as God's wrath sliced through it, ripping deep into the core, rendering it deformed. I lay there in terror, witnessing Nature's awesome strength and powerless to move. Acrid fumes filled the air close by, and the tree finally succumbed to its yawning wound and with one almighty crack, crashed to the ground, blocking the entrance to the cave.

I heard Don shout out,

"What the fuck was that?"

Slowly I gathered up my senses and realised Don was trapped inside the cave. When I explained the severity of the situation to him, and how he was entombed in the dark chamber, Don cheerily said,

"Oh well, at least I'm dry unlike you. Run along and tell my dad to come and get me."

Anyone else would have been petrified; not our Don. He saw the positive in everything. He'd assessed the situation and recognised the fact that he was relatively safe, dry, warm, and alive, and that I could scoot along and summon help. On the face of it he was right. Don hadn't got time for any fuss; he didn't make a drama out of a crisis. He just got on with what life threw at him, simple as that.

At a recent school reunion I bumped into Don and asked him why he'd lost all his amateur fights in the first round. It was obvious to most people, including his opponents, that he could kill them if he so wished; his street fighting was stuff of legend around South Yorkshire. Don explained to me that his uncle used to run an illegal betting syndicate, and every time Don took a dive, the pair of them made a few quid. Don was, and still is, an entrepreneur through and through.

Chapter 9
The Fat Liar

Over the years I've met some complete arseholes, but one that particularly sticks out in my mind was a guy we used to call Fugley; because he was both fat and ugly. This I could live with. His blatant lies on the other hand used to drive me to drink. If you could run the 100 metres in twelve seconds, he could walk it in ten. Whatever anyone did, Fugley told all and sundry that he did it better. I remember once telling him that I played for England at Wembley. He said he saw me do it! There was no beating him when it came to bragging rights. Fugley was a habitual, inveterate liar of the highest order.

I've met some romancers along my travels, I've bumped into jokers and people who are economical with the truth (I also fall into this latter category, along with my mate Smig), but downright liars are dangerous and cause a lot of trouble for people they associate with. My Grandad used to say to me:

"It takes two to lie son. One to lie and one to listen."

What this had to do with the price of fish is anyone's guess. My Grandad was a champion fibber, but not a liar; there is a big distinction. Fugley delighted in his fabrications such was his sad life. I've no idea whether or not he suffered from low self-esteem, or whether he was just a sadistic, sinister ratbag who loved bending the truth. He went on to become a top reporter in one of the national newspapers, which answers most people's questions. Fiction, as they say, is far more interesting than the truth.

Fugley's lies hit depths that other children couldn't begin to fathom. He once told me that his red blood corpuscles had eaten his liver and he only had minutes to live. By the time he'd finished explaining to me what corpuscles were, it had taken twenty bloody minutes, and he was still stood in front of me spouting off. Another beauty was when he told me he'd gotten hold of tickets for the space shuttle. He was so bent, that if this lad swallowed a nail, he'd shit a corkscrew. He couldn't lie straight in bed if he tried. His passion was pretending to be someone else, by either dressing up or assuming their identity. Whenever Fugley approached other children, they'd all burst into song simultaneously, singing,

"Seven foot, eight foot, nine foot ten, Fugley *exagging* once again."

Why he invented so much was beyond my comprehension. Not only did he possess the knack of falsifying everything and anything he ever spoke about, he also sported the biggest black-heads you'd ever seen. They were situated on the back of his neck, slightly below his ginger 'devil's curly hair'. They were as black as a gorilla's *gooleys* and as big as dustbin lids—bloody hell, now I've turned into Fugley! Chalkey once commented that Britain could solve the energy crisis by mounting derricks on Fugley's neck and drilling for oil; there must have been billions of gallons of crude under his skin.

Fugley was quite conscious about his oil reserves, and frequently got touchy when one of the gang mentioned them. On one occasion, the lads had been tormenting him all day, and come teatime, Fugley finally exploded. He turned into a whirling dervish, thrashing his arms round manically like a demented helicopter, hitting anyone who got in his way. One of the gang, Trotter, lost a tooth in the fracas. Being the diplomat of the group, I calmed the situation down, and took Fugley to one side to have a quiet word. Armed with my mediator's hat, I quelled the altercation, and peace was reinstated; well, for about five seconds. Chalkey, who had caused the entire rumpus in the first place, realising that harmony had been restored, looked straight into Fugley's eyes and said,

"Oil's well that ends well."

Like lighting a touchpaper to a rocket, Fugley went off with a massive bang, and the whole melee kicked off again. Chalkey had a knack of knowing just what to say and when to say it. It took an eternity to bring an end to the whole debacle, and induce a cessation of hostilities. Fugley was now sorely bruised on the outside as well as the inside. Looking at this lump of lard, snivelling and downtrodden, I suddenly felt a pang of guilt and put my arm around him.

"Hey Fuggs, come on mate and cheer up. You put up a good scrap against these five lads, and showed them what you're made of," I said, reassuring him somewhat.

"Yes Alf I suppose I did, but not as good as when I sparred with the great Henry Cooper, and knocked him out with one punch," was his reply.

Was there no end to his fantasies? I thought. Where does he get these yarns, and more importantly why? I'd exhibited my caring gentle nature to him, and his response was to carry on lying. Unbelievable, but that was Fugley. No matter how many good things he ever did, you could guarantee he'd soon let you down with a pack of lies. He was addicted to lying like most young boys are addicted to masturbation. I'm sure he never realised that all the lads thought he was a complete prick; he still persisted in bending the truth. It never impressed anyone, not until we all got caught at Mortimer Fothergill's party one evening.

Mortimer Fothergill, or 'Mo-Fo' as he was affectionately referred to, came from an affluent family in Tickhill, a posh village some four miles from Maltby. Mortimer had been privately educated, and was one of the 'old school' so to speak. His grandfather, Major Bassington-French Mortimer was the local landowner, and wildly eccentric. Mortimer would travel to the school bus stop on a pony and trap each morning, armed with a leather briefcase and sporting a cravat. He looked a bit of a pillock, but underneath this outlandish garb there was a real nice kid. He never once lauded his privileged background, and always shared his beer and cider, pilfered from his grandfather's cabinet. He said that he couldn't help being brought up into vast wealth, and to him money meant nothing. What a load of shite we all thought. Money when you're poor means everything, and due to this we were at his house at every opportunity. Mo-Fo became our new best mate over night, such was our collective shallowness.

Following his successful O'level results (GCSE's in new money), Mo-Fo decided to throw a party at his mansion; me and the lads were all invited. This was our equivalent of Hollywood and we were all excited to fever pitch. For the main guests there would be a veritable feast of pheasant, quail eggs, truffles and champagne, and for us lot, turkey-buzzard *sarnies* and coke! Mo's grandfather didn't approve of the "*Maltby riff-raff*" as he referred to us, and felt that his grandson should mix with more suitable children who were a little less interbred. Fortunately for us, Mo-Fo ignored his advice and happily befriended us all.

On the evening of the big party, I met up with my mates on Queen's Corner, and proceeded to the local off-license to load up with cheap beer and cider. We were sixteen years old and under the legal age to purchase alcohol, but our accommodating off-license owner always overlooked this minor point, and duly served us with whatever we desired. Money was tight, so it was always Kestrel lager, Zum-Zider (a potent mixture of Cornish cider and meths), and Bull's Blood for Chalkey. A quick sprint down to the Crags, slurp the said booze as quickly as humanly possible and we were merrily on our way to the festivities. Back then, taxis were unheard of in the area and nobody could have afforded one anyway. One hour and four miles later we arrived in Tickhill; a little the worse for wear, and looking somewhat dishevelled. Within one more hour, Chalkey had caused three more fights and thrown up, Sal had been arrested for pissing in the middle of the road, and Russ was rubbing the face of a two pence coin for good luck.

Tickhill was and still is a beautiful village, though some people now refer to it as a town. Folks who live there say that the only downside to Tickhill is that you have to travel through Maltby to get to it. Tickhill boasts its own castle, a large thirteenth century parish church, and a butter cross. For the historians amongst you this is great; to us teenagers, the only thing that interested us in Tickhill, apart from Mo's swanky pad, was that the place had an abundance of pubs.

Getting served in pubs under the legal age of eighteen posed somewhat of a problem for me and my mates. The fact that none of us looked older than fourteen didn't help matters. Fortunately for us back then though, ID cards didn't exist, and there was no way on earth that the police would get off their fat idle arses to travel out to a village and check the pubs for underage drinkers. Not to be fazed by such a dilemma, we came up with a devious plan. I decided that to make myself look more grown up, I would enter the hostelry smoking a pipe. This I did and I eventually got served, but only after the barmaid stopped pissing her sides at me. Smig followed me in wearing a tail-coat and flat cap combination (sort of opera-meets-badger-baiter), and finally Russ flounced in dressed as his Aunty Sheila. Chalkey was still outside being sick. When I think of this now, we must have looked like a bunch of escapees from Rampton Mental Home.

Several pints later we were staggering our way over to Mo's for the shindig.

Mo's palace was out of this world; turrets, bell tower, ornamental lake, folly, you name it, he had it. As we crunched our way through the gravel that led to the front doors, we were met by the man-servant of the house, Doug, who had a face like a horse's arse. He was a local man in his seventies, extremely short-sighted, with an irritating pseudo-posh accent.

"Good evening gentlemen. The bins are around the back of the house if you please," he said condescendingly.

Chalkey reeled up towards him, and fell into his arms.

"Me and you against the world mate, the bastards," he slurred, knocking him over.

Doug crashed to the ground, with Chalkey floundering on top of him. Quick thinking Russ rushed to Doug's assistance, and helped the elderly butler to his feet.

"Why you look handsome tonight Doug, so much so I could eat you," Russ uttered into his ear.

At this point you have to remember Russ was attired as a woman; false boobs, earrings, stilettos, the works. Doug regained his senses, and wiped his eyes. Who was this nubile goddess whispering sweet nothings into his lug-holes? Doug composed himself and ushered us into the main house, clinging to Russ like a limpet. He thought he was in for a bit of *afters* following the party, with what he hoped was a licentious whore—happy days all round. We were in, and Doug had pulled. To give Russ his credit, he played a blinder. As Doug brushed past me I distinctly heard him say,

"If her body is a temple, I'm a religious fanatic."

Stumbling buffoonlike into the soiree, the first thing to attract my attention was the number of girls. I was greeted with wall-to-wall *totty*—adolescent babes waiting to be whisked off to the boudoirs that beckoned aloft. My first action was to clean up my appearance in the kitchen, whilst simultaneously helping myself to a flagon of ale. Back in the '70s, our choice of stimulant was alcohol. Drugs didn't come into the equation. The only time I ever experimented with narcotics was when I was eighteen, and sniffed sellotape. Filling a pint pot with Brew Ten bitter I sauntered into the main dining hall. *Crikey Moses*, I'd never seen so much food in my young life. Instinct kicked in, and I immediately forgot about the crumpet, and started to fill my pockets with pork pies. Well it was going to be a late and long trek home, and a strapping lad needs his sustenance, I reasoned.

From the corner of the hall Doug was watching my every move. Because he was as blind as a bat from close quarters, I hadn't factored in that from a distance he had the eyesight of a peregrine falcon. He briskly marched over to me with that "I'm going to throw you out on your arse" look etched across his mug. Russ, monitoring the situation, swiftly interjected and blocked off his means of access.

"Doug, would you like to park your car in my garage?" Russ whispered into Doug's jug ear.

On hearing these words of encouragement, Doug concentrated his efforts and thoughts on Russ, whose make-up had been reapplied to make him look even more like Dame Edna Everage. With Doug now off my trail I made a speedy retreat, and quite by accident found myself in one of the upstairs bedrooms with some toffee-nose damsel who certainly was in distress. She was sobbing uncontrollably about not having a boyfriend at such a wonderful party, and what a waste it would be for all concerned. Like any typical lad, I was attentive, caring, understanding, sympathetic, and yes, focused on the goodies she had on offer. Taking control of the situation to ease her pain and sorrow, I suggested that we got undressed and into bed to try to resolve the problems first hand. Seemingly, she thought my proposition was top drawer, and duly clambered into the sack, all naked and everything.

I suddenly realised that, like the lyrics to the old Rod Stewart song 'Tonight's the night', my cherry was ready to be popped. I was overcome with excitement, and started to experience butterflies in my stomach. The beer had kicked in, but I was still ready to give my debut performance a go, and a *rogering* awaited my damsel. I divested myself of my attire apart from my vivid red Y-front undies, and slipped into the silky sheets. This was it Alfie-Boy, I was thinking, my duck was about to be broken, regardless of the girl's dilemma. It was my reckoning that she needed a shoulder to cry on, and I needed to break the ice.

As I slowly cradled my newfound love in my arms, the door burst open; like a raging elephant, Mo's grandfather stormed in armed with his shotgun. He flicked the lights on, and I squinted to try to focus on what was happening. Like waking from a dream, it took me several seconds to get my bearings. When I came to my senses I realised all too quickly that I was staring down the barrel of a twelve bore, which I can tell you is no fun at all. My companion stayed under the sheets, so I was left alone to face my captor. I could clearly see the whites of his eyes, inside a maniac's face, vermillion in colour with puffed out cheeks. This was it I thought, my short existence was about to come to a bloody end. And I'd not even scored.

"What the dickens do you think you're doing with my niece you bounder? Better come up with a jolly sound reason you oik, or your balls will be adorning my Picasso on that wall!" Fothergill Senior bellowed.

Just when you think it couldn't get any worse, at that precise moment my bedmate slipped her hand into my underpants, probably just to keep it warm. It was the last thing I needed, what with Major Fothergill about to blast my plums into next week; it did feel kind of nice though. Before I could protest my innocence, Fugley bounded into the bedroom dressed as what I can only describe as a cross between Sherlock Holmes and Dixon of Dock Green, complete with whistle and truncheon.

"Ha, Major, I can see you've apprehended our hairy pie rustler. Well done old boy, I will take it from here," Fugley said in a rather unusual deep voice, trying to sound all policemanlike.

Fugley then noticed the gun.

"What have we here then Major? Have you a license for that weapon? My, my, I think I may have to detain you and take you down to the station for further questioning. I'm pretty sure that this is the same gun used in the post office robbery last week in Braithwell that I'm investigating," Fugley said.

What the shit was Fugley up to? His lies were legendary, but impersonating a police officer was a very serious offence. He was definitely overstepping the mark with this disguise, especially with the Major. Had he lost all his senses? Fothergill stopped in his tracks, and lowered the blunderbuss.

"Who the hell are you supposed to be?" the Major yelled.

"Never mind who I am sir drop your weapon and turn to face the Picasso please," Fugley replied.

It was like being in a surreal Radio 4 afternoon play; way beyond my comprehension, and too much to absorb. Unbelievably, the Major cocked his gun, laid it on the floor, and turned to face the wall. Fugley tapped me on the back of the head and winked, pointing his truncheon in the direction of the door. I didn't need any more hints, and I set off from the scene of the crime like the clappers, neither bothering to get dressed or look back. Lord knows what my sweetheart thought of my cowardice, but I wanted to keep my bollocks intact for a few more years. Sex could wait.

Chapter 10
Goodbye Grandad

Having bummed around all summer, relationships began to get strained at home and I was forced into looking for a job. Money was still tight, but I felt I didn't need cash; I could easily live off fresh air. Ha, the innocence and ignorance of youth. Whenever I was skint, Grandad always stumped up a few bob to keep me solvent. I in turn visited him every weekend, taking my mates with me. We'd get his coal in, chop logs into firewood, and tidy his garden up. We loved his company and he loved ours. Grandad always had a joke or two up his sleeve, and my mates thought the world of him.

During this period I began to notice a deterioration in his health, which came on quite rapidly. He'd had a heart attack several years earlier, but now his angina attacks were getting more severe. Watching my hero go downhill was most unpleasant and upsetting. He became house-bound, and found great difficulty in walking. We brought his bed downstairs for ease and convenience, and spent many a Saturday night with him, watching films featuring the Marx Brothers into the late hours. Craig and I would put up Z-beds at the side of his divan, and sleep in the front room with him. We would play dominoes, cards, do crosswords, and generally fart about.

Grandad wasn't a Catholic like me. He didn't believe in anything. He was a stoic and proud man who'd grafted all his life down the pit, and quenched his raging thirst with a flagon or two of ale most days. He was a simple chap who loved his football, cricket and horse racing. I recall him once telling me,

"Alf, men only like two things, sex and sport."

When I come to think about this, he's not far wrong, but I must say, I once met a guy who didn't like sex. I also remember Grandad picking me up for throwing leftover food from my plate onto the fire. He accused me of feeding the devil. When I asked him why he didn't believe in God, but thought the devil existed, he just laughed and gave me a wicked stare. Other colourful memories I have of him were washing his face in the kitchen sink, pouring tea from his cup into his saucer then drinking it, cutting bread and scraping the crumbs into his hands then eating them, wearing big daft braces, and most of all blaming the dog for his own incessant farts.

Grandad was also quite a philosopher. Spending so much time bedridden and housebound had given him plenty of time to reflect on life. One afternoon, I found him stood at the back door looking into his sparse and weed-filled garden, admiring Nature and all her beauty. His next door neighbour was frantically ripping out the weeds that had grown into his beautiful garden from my Grandad's, cursing away under his breath as he was doing it.

"Now then Harry, don't deplete Nature's resources. Learn from the honey bee, take only what you need," Grandad chipped in.

Harry's reply ended with the word "off".

If Grandad was still living now, he would have definitely been a 'Saga-lout' such was his sense of humour and outlook on life. Always forthcoming with a joke or two, and always seeing the funny side of things, he never dropped his smile, even when struck down with his serious illness. He'd be sat up in bed coughing his lungs up and struggling for breath one minute, and the next he'd be cracking a joke. Inadvertently, I'd often be part of one of his funnies without knowing it. One evening I heard a knock at the door and on answering it was greeted by the rent man.

"Grandad, there's a man at the door with a bald head," I shouted.

"Tell him I've already got one," was Grandad's reply.

As I reflect back on my youth, I've come to realise what a huge influence my Grandad had on me. He taught me to laugh in the face of adversity, mock danger and ridicule religion. He was a bugger. When I was growing up 'bugger' was a word we associated with being naughty. Another expression often heard in my youth was "bugger up the backs". Looking at this expression now in the cold light of day, I think I'll swiftly move on.

The wire fence separating my Grandad's back yard and Harry Fox's was antiquated and dilapidated at best. Harry had told Grandad on numerous occasions that it was his responsibility to maintain and repair the fence; Grandad agreed in principle but never actually did anything about it. Whisky, Grandad's dog, would stray onto Harry's vegetable patch and provide a fresh dollop of dog shit on his cabbages and carrots on a daily basis. After several weeks of this illicit muck-spreading, Harry finally cracked and put up a new fence. When he knocked the nail into the final post, Grandad ambled out to admire Harry's handiwork. After shaking the fence to check for sturdiness, Grandad congratulated his neighbour on a fine job. Harry quickly jumped to his feet and presented him a bill for £30 for the timber and nails. Grandad took one look at it, then handed it straight back to Harry saying,

"That's not a bad price old boy. You must have driven a hard bargain with the timber merchant. Well done."

At this remark, my Grandad turned tail and slowly made his way back into the kitchen, never for an instant thinking of parting with any of his money. In total disbelief at my Grandad's lack of contribution, Harry shook his head, and made his way wearily back indoors, cursing more loudly this time. The new fence looked fine and certainly lifted the garden. About half way down its length the fence curved around a mature apple tree, which sat in Harry's garden, but lurched over into my Grandad's, due to the top section of the tree having been grafted on at some earlier stage of its life.

If you stood directly beside the fence and looked down its length, you could clearly see that the bottom three feet of the tree trunk grew in Harry's patch, whilst virtually the remainder of the trunk and canopy nestled over my Grandad's. Technically the tree was Harry's, as his father had planted it many years before. This didn't pose a problem between the two parties—until harvesting the crop in late September each year.

Harry would get up at dawn, sneak out into the garden armed with a long clothes pole with a bag attached to the end of it. He would then knock the branches that the apples were attached to with the end of the pole, and the fruit would fall into the bag below. An ingenious and simple device which proved very effective in the scrumping stakes. Watching Harry straining over the perimeter fence trying desperately to bag all the apples that hung over Grandad's garden was entertainment at its bloody best.

Poor old Harry was desperate to collect every apple that the tree had to offer, though why he didn't just come to an agreement with Grandad over the spoils was beyond me. After several gruelling hours, Harry had amassed a shed load of Bramleys and was looking rather content, if not a little smug with himself. With the tree stripped bare, like a plague of locusts had descended on it, Harry sat beneath its gnarled branches and wiped the sweat from his brow.

Grandad, who like me had been watching the mornings activities, opened the bedroom window and called out,

"Sitting under a tree gives a man peace and enlightenment. The trouble with folk today is that they have disconnected themselves from the natural world. They should make peace with the Earth, what it is, and not what they can take from it. Now put those fucking apples back or I'll kick the shit out of you. Good morning."

Grandad had the knack of being philosophical and direct. It's these colourful anecdotes that make me still laugh out loud to this day. Even when his illness was getting the better of him, he never let his neighbour beat him.

The problem with Grandad's illness was the way in which it was winning the battle; Grandad began to suffer more and more each day. Whenever I visited and asked him if he needed anything, the answer was always the same: "A gun and one bullet." Grandad was unlike most men as he didn't moan about his condition. He just put up with it. Looking into his eyes I could sense the pain and agony he was suffering; the thing that upset me the most was not being able to do anything. I felt hopeless, but I'm sure just being there helped in a small way. I can still picture him in his kitchen sat in his special chair, white string vest on stained with snuff, Bush radio on the mantelpiece playing old songs, and the sound of a clock ticking in the background. Each tick taking him closer to his maker.

Watching a man slowly die is horrendous. When it's someone you love dearly and depend on for most things, it's heart-breaking. There was absolutely nothing I could do to relieve his pain and suffering. I felt pathetic, and began to question why God would do this to him, and then began to question my own faith. Grandad was struck down in his early sixties, which is no age at all, especially with people living well into their eighties now. I knew that working down a mine, eating coal dust for breakfast, and having a diet that consisted of fried food and beer doesn't help the old arteries, but he was a good man who deserved to get more out of life. The thing that really got to me was that even on his death bed, I thought that he would survive and get better; it was the only thing I was optimistic about in my youth. He couldn't die; I wouldn't let it happen.

One evening, I received the news that he'd passed away. The shock was too much to bear, and I collapsed. I remember feeling hollow and numb. When Grandad died, a big part of me died also. I couldn't take it in; it was all too overpowering and tragic. I knew Craig felt the same, but he was always better at hiding his emotions. I went to pieces. Loneliness, emptiness, desolation, isolation, they all figured in my thoughts. Now I would have no one to turn to, no one in my corner to look after me. Grandad was always there listening to me. He made me feel special, however rubbish I actually was at dealing with life. He made me laugh, but most importantly, he loved me.

Writing this now is extremely difficult for me, as I knew it would be. They say death is a continuum of life. Try telling that to a sixteen-year-old who felt he'd lost everything. Back in the '70s, counselling was in its infancy, and people just had to face up to their trials and tribulations, and deal with them alone. Children and adolescents are vulnerable and need help and support. I was told to "buck up, and get on with it. Life's crap and then you die." You can imagine how I felt hearing such words of sympathy.

Due to Nan being a Catholic, Grandad was laid to rest in an open coffin in her front room, so the family could pay their last respects. The family insisted on me seeing him one last time to remember him. I resisted, but eventually caved in to the pressure, and I honestly wish I hadn't. What I saw lying there in that ornamental wooden box was not my Grandad. He didn't even look like him. Grandad would have been sat up for a start, smiling with a twinkle in his eye, ready to share a joke. He would have been wearing his vest and braces, and the radio would have been playing. Alas, none of this greeted me, only silence, deathly silence...

I was stunned and speechless; and couldn't move a muscle, even though I was desperate to leave. One of my uncles realised my predicament and ushered me outside. I remember shrugging him off, running like a steam train down the cinderpath, not stopping at the junction between High Street and Millindale. Fortunately back then, the roads were a lot less busy, but I still could have ended my own life there and then because of how upset I was. I kept running, until I reached Roche Abbey, and collapsed onto the ground sobbing uncontrollably, cursing God for what he'd taken from me, and wanting to fight the world. I was angry and bitter and wanted revenge; revenge against the Almighty.

Eventually after several hours I calmed down, but couldn't release my pent-up emotions. I kicked the Abbey walls, and stubbed my toe in the process causing me to scream out in pain. The gamekeeper, old 'One Eye and a Ball of Chalk' was alerted to my cries, and wandered over to me to see what all the commotion was about. He knew my Grandad had passed away, and passed on his condolences.

He reassured me that my Grandad might have left this Earth, but would live on through me. On hearing this I began to feel a little better. He also went on to add how lucky I was to have known such a great bloke and shared so many happy memories with him. 'One Eye' was usually a complete bastard, but on this occasion I couldn't have wished for anyone better to be comforting me. What he said made sense, and he certainly made me realise what a special person my Grandad was. Time is indeed a great healer, but my goodness it took a very long time for me to heal the wounds of losing my best mate—Grandad.

A few years ago, at my Nan's *145*th birthday party, my Uncle Jim came in to the room, took one look at me, and stopped dead in his tracks. He looked shocked and somewhat shaken. When I asked him what was wrong, he had to sit down to catch his breath and collect his thoughts.

"By gum Alf, you're the spitting image of your Grandad."

I'm not a family man, never have been, never will be, but hearing those words made me smile, both on the outside and on the inside. It was the ultimate compliment he could have given me. He then went on to say,

"Fuck me, where's all your hair gone?"

Cheeky bastard, I thought.

Chapter 11
Viva Espagna

Throughout the 1970s Britain suffered a decade of strikes involving miners, postal workers and even dustmen. As the decade drew to a close the Great British public endured the 'winter of discontent' when ITV went off air for five months. I remember Margaret Thatcher getting elected as Prime Minister in May 1979, and thinking what a complete set of twats the Labour party was for allowing a woman to oust them out of power by screwing up the country, such was my sexist and political ignorance; for God's sake, she didn't even have big tits!

Space hoppers, shoe-box cassette recorders, colour television, platform shoes; the '70s for me were great, but I was still *pink-lint* and didn't have a pot to piss in. Britain lost its greatness and like me, was going nowhere, or so it seemed at the time. It was, however, an era of global travel when air travel became cheaper and accessible to the masses. Normal thick Northern bastards like me had a chance to fly all over the world, and I was given the opportunity to holiday in Spain for two weeks with Smig and his family. The fortnight cost me a full £36 which seemed achievable and attainable, even by my standards. I scraped the coppers together by selling my bike and my brother's arse to uncle Nesbit—there is another complete chapter here, but I'll spare Craig's blushes and leave it for another day.

Uncle Nesbit was described as a mentalist; that is someone who utilises mental acuity, hypnosis and/or suggestion. What a load of bollocks! He was just simply fucking mental, with a slight bent for chastising young boys with his hand on their bare arses for no apparent reason.

Being offered a chance to go abroad was both exciting and very frightening. I suddenly realised that I was shit-scared of flying, something that I've only recently overcome. Having friends who were luxuriating in foreign climes, and with the cost of package holidays so inexpensive and fashionable, I had no choice but to say yes to Smig. Prior to me going away we had evenings of intense excitement, planning how many senoritas we were going to shag in Spain, whilst getting arseholed on Brew-Ten bitter in the Toll Bar. The anticipation of a fortnight in the sun can get the better of you, and be thoroughly enjoyed to the max many times over before the actual event.

My initial apprehension about flying soon began to turn to dread and fear, and to combat this I started drinking more to quell my anxiety. During the weeks leading up to the flight I couldn't sleep, which was nothing out of the ordinary for an insomniac. Lying in bed thinking of shagging my neighbour's daughter was normal; lying in the sack contemplating death was something totally new to me. It was at this point in my short life that my fear turned into major anxiety, palpitations and cold sweats, which has affected me ever since. A popular record at this time was 'I Will Survive' by Gloria Gaynor; I was hoping that would become my theme tune for the duration.

The most popular destinations in the package holiday boom of the '70s were the Spanish Costas and Greece. Smig's family opted for Spain as the flight time was shorter. Our resort was *San Antonio de Colonic-Irrigation,* or something similar sounding. It was off the beaten track with no 'kiss-me-quick' hats in sight. It did sell the mandatory big daft sombreros and stuffed donkeys though; I bought both, and still treasure them dearly.

The dilemma I found myself in—going or not going, fear versus excitement—started to get the better of me so I sought the advice of Smig's dad Harold, who was a seasoned overseas traveller.

"Don't worry Alf, we're flying on Buddy Holly Airlines, and the pilot is a personal friend of mine. It's incredible that he can fly a plane at all with him being totally blind," he assured me.

"Totally blind?" I screamed back at him.

"Yes, since birth apparently," Harold went on to say.

"How does he know when to take off then?" I asked, my voice now trembling with fear.

"He just waits for all the passengers to yell 'fuckin hell'," he replied.

I realised that Harold was pissing up my back whilst telling me it was raining. Harold was a character who liked playing jokes; he also plied the trade of hunch and hearsay, commonly known as gossip.

No matter how much I deliberated on the subject of flying, the holiday was booked and there was no looking back. I remember downing a couple of horse tranquillisers washed down with a few pints, prior to leaving the airport. The flight was then nothing more than a blur. Upon arrival, Harold hailed two taxis and we trundled off into the Spanish night, heading for Villa Frigmorole on the outskirts of town. Even though I was somewhat out of it, I recall Smig and Reg hurling expletives at the driver, whilst simultaneously laughing and patting him on the back, so as not to draw too much attention to their spurious and libellous remarks about the *grasiento, apestoso, dago bastardo.*

The villa had seen better days, and so had I. Still spaced out, I unpacked by putting my suit-case into the wardrobe, brushed my teeth and joined the lads to visit the local disco. We were the only English in the venue; the rest of the young inhabitants looked bronzed and distinctly foreign. My mate Reg was a ringer for the singer Rod Stewart, and within minutes inside the place he had girls all over him. To add to his charm, he'd broken his arm the week before we flew, so he looked all pathetic and helpless, like men do when they're scheming to get inside a female's knickers. He was drowning happily in their lavish attention, whilst Smig and I were locked in an intense eye-staring competition with about fifty Spanish boys, all extremely pissed off at Reg and his new found harem. I suggested to Smig that we made a sharp exit as I had a fair idea what was about to erupt. Within seconds of leaving the disco by the back doors, we were surrounded by what seemed like a thousand very irate dagos, baying for our blood. I felt like a bull being goaded by umpteen matadors, only these guys had bigger swords.

The situation was dire, but I can remember thinking bollocks to this for a game of soldiers, and just started laying into them. Surprisingly they dropped like flies, Spanish flies at that, and things suddenly didn't look too bad. That was until another swarm of the dirty, greasy bastards appeared from around the corner. Knackered from Spanish teenagers running into my fists, Smig alerted me to the fact that he'd hit a lad so hard, he'd broken his hand; he therefore retired from the gladiatorial arena leaving me on my *Jack Jones*.

The Spanish lads didn't seem to know when to quit, and I was quickly tiring out. When another ten or so bigger lads decided to join in, I began to think that my days in Spain would amount to one. As I gasped for breath, the night air was then filled with the sound of screaming sirens, heading straight in our direction. I recall thinking to myself that getting into a ruck with teenagers was one thing, but coming up against the Spanish police was quite another. Not being able to effectively communicate with Spanish people, my chances of escaping from foreign law enforcement were very slim indeed. The idea of being locked up in a Spanish hell-hole and being constantly bummed by a filthy Spaniard didn't appeal to me. The term '*bobbin from a gibbet*' also filled my mind.

Me and my two buddies quickly scarpered down a dark alley, and hid inside some enormous dustbins.

As dawn broke, we gingerly made our way home. The streets were minus any citizens and as silent as death. Our pace began to pick up, and before too long we reached the sanctuary of our villa, to be met outside by a fearsome looking Harold.

Harold wasn't a happy bunny, and I could see we were about to get a mighty tongue-lashing. As I ventured closer to him, I noticed to my surprise that he was still dressed in his pyjamas. This may seem trivial to most folk, but Harold's 'PJs' were baby-blue with a massive felt embroidered letter 'E' on the left pyjama top pocket. It was strikingly odd. I was curious to know the reason, so I plucked up courage and asked him.

"Hey Harold, what does the letter 'E' stand for?"

"What? Oh that; it stands for elephant, you moronic bastard," he snapped back at me.

Bizarre answer, I thought at the time, and like an elephant, I've never forgot it. After the bollocking, we hit the sack. I was awoken at noon by Smig moaning and groaning about how his hand was hurting.

"For fuck's sake Smig, it's probably broken. Stop whinging and get back to sleep. You can sort it out later," I said, all sympathetic and caring-like.

"It is broken Alf, and I think I'm going to have to go to hospital," he replied, sobbing uncontrollably like the pathetic hypochondriac we all knew he was.

Unfortunately for once he was right; his hand was definitely broken. The hospital staff cared for Smig even less than me, and after seven hours, he was bandaged up to match Reg and packed on his way. Harold was mortified at what the Spanish doctor charged him. I think it would have been cheaper to have him put down. When we arrived back at 'Frigmarole' Reg and Smig went back to bed, leaving Harold and I to head out to the town to fetch provisions.

Harold was a real character; totally nuts. He was a squat man, solid as a rock and daft as a brush. Harold wasn't the sharpest tool in the box. I recall him once tinting his car windows so people couldn't see into the vehicle; he was on the run from the law at the time. The problem was that when he'd finished the job, he couldn't see out from inside the car but everyone else could see in! He also once purchased some dodgy one-pound coins for a *tenne*r each! His best quip was made to a local farmer. Harold, a butcher by trade, was admiring the farmer's beasts. The farmer notified him that unfortunately all his cattle were suffering from blue-tongue. Harold, somewhat bemused said,

"Bloody hell mate, how technology has moved on. I didn't realise cows had mobiles."

Arriving at 'El Supermercado' we were astonished to discover that inside it possessed a bar adjacent the checkout counter. Harold suggested that we "slaked the dust" first and had a few glasses. Sounded pretty good to me, and three hours later, both worse for wear, we were both escorted off the premises for lewd and crude behaviour. Having forgotten entirely about getting the provisions for his family, we stumbled into a bar for more Sangria, which we'd now developed a taste for.

My whole concept of time vanished, as did my sense of reasoning, due to the alcohol kicking in and the *red mist* descending over me. Having only just got out of one scrape the night before, I now found myself in another, with an elderly Spanish lady, who must have been ninety if a day. She accused me of fondling her maracas, the lying bitch. She also intimated that I was after giving her one. Even though I was half-cut at the time, I remember thinking to myself that if I'd had sex with such an old turkey, she would have been so dry down below, the friction caused would have set her on fire. She then had the bare faced cheek to accuse me of standing on her nipples whilst I was holding a can of lager at arm's length and directing a jet of the amber nectar into my mouth. I'm sure I heard someone call her 'Martini', meaning any time, any place, anywhere. Why she picked on me was anyone's guess, but she did. Within minutes the police had arrived at the bar and I was arrested.

I was whisked off down to the station and interrogated for several hours; this included being stripped naked and *probed*. Not the most pleasant feeling I've experienced, but one I will treasure for the rest of my life. I confessed to everything, from causing the Spanish Civil War, to being a Basque separatist. I even told them that I actually enjoyed paella, which from my point of view, was my biggest lie that day. I was incarcerated for the remainder of the vacation, and only released when Harold slipped one of the screws a fistful of pesetas. I still owe him some of this fine, but the chance of him remembering or finding out about it from this book are as about as remote as me growing a full head of hair.

Over the past few months I've been enrolled on a course at my local college, learning conversational Spanish. The tutor is a little strange, but apparently I'm coming on smashing. I now know that the Spanish for Phillips screwdriver is *destornillador de estrella*, and fuse box is *la caja de fusible*. Useful if you're an electrician, but useless when ordering extras in a brothel.

Chapter 12
Get A Proper Job, You Fat Slut

With Grandad sadly departed and the summer holidays drawing to an end, I was under tremendous pressure at home to find a job and earn my keep. (I've never been afraid of hard work, and my wife tells me that I could find work in an empty room, but trying to find a job that suits me is a really difficult task.) Having left the lower sixth, halfway through my 'A' levels, the only qualifications I had were the five olives from De La Salle; I'd virtually wasted my year at comprehensive buggering around.

One evening in the local chippie, I'd bumped into Chalkey, who informed me that he'd started work at British Steel as a metallurgist. I hadn't a bloody clue what one of those was, but it sounded impressive, and that was good enough for me. The bonus, if I got the job, would be that I would be reunited with my old mate. I got hold of an application form, and before you could say "fanny-tickler" I was interviewed and secured the post.

My location for work was Templeborough, an industrial suburb of Rotherham, which once again happened to be two bus rides from Maltby; one to Rotherham and one to my place of work. It reminded me of my long, boring journeys to De La Salle a year earlier, but at least I wouldn't be doing exams this time, or so I thought. The atmosphere on the bus was completely different from what I was used to. There were no schoolkids for a start, and everyone seemed depressed. After several weeks at work I began to feel exactly the same and wore the same lifeless expression. I must admit, having a proper job—apprentice metallurgist—did feel kind of strange.

When I first arrived at work, I presumed that I'd be working with Chalkey, so I just joined him in one of his classes. Within seconds we were back messing around and playing the fool like the good old days. An instructor then entered the room, and immediately informed me that I was wanted at the other end of the complex; I was to join another group of trainees. I was mortified. Traipsing over to my new set-up, I felt somewhat forlorn and despondent.

Eventually I entered a small dark room to be greeted by fourteen other new recruits, two of them being the fairer of the species. Things were beginning to look up, and all thoughts of Chalkey disappeared. Both the girls were extremely bright and good looking. To top it all, they were both single. I immediately went into my class clown routine, but got nowhere. These two dollies were intelligent, that was the big difference. I wasn't used to being around such intellect (no disrespect to my mates and previous girlfriends), and I suddenly realised I was out of my depth.

To compound matters, my new trainer informed us that we would be spending the first three months at Richmond College the very next week, to do a crash course in 'Iron and Steel Technology'. Shit I thought, I've just left school to stop doing exams and the sort, and here I am, first day in a new job being told I am on a release-course at college for three months. The added pressure was that at the end of the intense, quick semester there was an exam which you had to pass, or you'd be sacked.

I've always hated exams. I still have recurring nightmares about them and not having done enough revision. So in a nut-shell, I started a new career without my best mate, back at college, and surrounded by girls who thought I wasn't funny. What had I let myself in for? This felt like the pits for me. That very evening, when I returned home, I immediately got an application form to join the Civil Service. I thought that working for the government would be a far cleaner, easier job, with more prospects—and less intellectual girls.

My time at Richmond College flew by, and was I must admit, quite enjoyable. I'd heard nothing from the Civil Service, so gave it up for lost. Surprisingly, I passed my exam; I got 69% and came joint bottom of the class with a boy nicknamed Pugg. College was a laugh, and during those three months I broke my duck in the sex stakes with a girl from Taiwan. I won't go into graphic detail as I only lasted thirty-five seconds, but I did quite enjoy the experience and get a taste for it—rather fishy if I remember rightly. Girls began to take over my life, and I lurched from one bad relationship to another. I got easily bored; commitment wasn't for me—especially with girls who finished with me on the first date.

Back at Templeborough, having passed my exam, I now found myself working on the shop floor. My superior was a guy named Burkie; Fugley must have been his love-child, such were his blatant lies. Another bonus for me at this time was that I was reunited with Chalkey again. He had been assigned to my group with Pugg. Burkie was a first-class prick, but I loved working with him, just for his stories. He once told us about swimming in a 'rift-valley' in Ravenfield with thirty naked women. He said he had only managed to have sex with twenty-five of them before he'd *"jacked off, backed off and fucked the other three"*. His lies were spectacular. He was in a different league to Fugley, and I couldn't get enough of being in his company. With regard to the 'rift valley' scenario, the largest freshwater lakes in the world are located in rift valleys. Ravenfield is a tiny hamlet with a puddle at one end, is as flat as a fart, and certainly doesn't possess a rift valley. The word *'rift'* means an estrangement or separation— like that of Burkie's strange mind was from the rest of reality.

Another classic from Burkie was when he went scuba-diving in Maltby Beck, and caught a sturgeon with his spear gun. The stream is only a foot deep and the only life it supports is minnows and bull-heads. It's polluted to such an extent that all water life is either deformed or dead. I actually felt sorry for the guy because this was his only way of being able to impress anyone.

For some reason or another though, Chalkey despised him with a passion. It was true that Burkie could spin a good yarn, and this I could easily deal with, but he had another little irritating habit of telling our ultimate superior every minor thing we did wrong. He was a *telltale-tit*. This gave him a sense of power, like the sneak in the playground feels when feeding information to bullies for their sadistic pleasure. He delighted at our misdemeanours and errors whilst carrying out our respective work tasks.

One particular job given to me was to simply transport a container carrying a load of steel from one part of a room to another for analysis. I was equipped with my personal protection equipment, and long steel tongs to move the vessel approximately ten feet. Sounds straightforward enough, and indeed it was for most people; not me though. I started to laugh and dropped the entire contents onto the floor, jeopardising a full week's work. Chalkey realised my plight and rushed to help me, saying if we brushed the ashes back into the container, no one would ever be any the wiser.

Sat in the wings was Burkie, who witnessing my dilemma firsthand, set off in the direction of the manager's office like a rat up a drainpipe. He couldn't wait to break the bad news to the gaffer and drop me in it. The boss went ballistic, and I was given a written warning there and then. Apparently my inadequacy had cost British Steel a full shift amounting to several thousand pounds, which was a small fortune back then. To this day I still don't know whether the pair of them were bullshitting me, but it certainly knocked my duck off. On the bus home that same night, Chalkey and I hatched a plan to get revenge on Burkie. He'd been having it all his way, so we had to redress the balance.

Next day, me and Chalks got an earlier bus to work. On arrival, we stripped down stark-bollock naked, apart from our steel-capped boots and hard hats. We made our way into the workshop where the tensile testing machine was sited. Catching Burkie out of the corner of my eye, I tipped Chalks the wink, and we knelt down simultaneously and started chanting at the machine in *foreign tongues*. On spying this spectacle, Burkie set off to fetch the gaffer. We had anticipated his every move, and by the time Burkie and our boss turned up, we had slipped our overalls back on and were frantically sweeping the shop floor, whistling merrily in the process.

"What's the problem gaffer?" I said, noticing his puzzled expression.

"Oh, erm, erm nothing lads. Good job, keep it up. Burke, into my office now!" he yelled.

Ten minutes later, Burkie sauntered into the workshop, with a face like a slapped arse. He'd obviously had a right rollicking. In the interval, Chalkey and I had again de-robed and were knelt in front of the machine, chanting and bowing in adoration. Burkie wiped his eyes, and turned around, making his way back to the manager's office. Like in the film 'Groundhog Day' once again the manager and Burkie reappeared on the scene, only this time to observe Chalks and me dusting the machinery down, fully clothed.

"Hey boss, you look a little bemused, what's the matter?" Chalkey piped up.

The look on Burkie's face was a picture. The gaffer shook his head at Burkie and suggested he visit the firm's nurse right away. He then pulled me over and said,

"Alf, have you noticed anything strange about Burkie over the past few days?"

"Well yes I have, but I didn't want to drop him in it. He's been worshipping at the foot of the tensile testing machine every morning, stark naked and chanting something or another. I think he's cracking up under the strain of the job. Maybe he needs a transfer?" I said innocently.

"On the face of it Alf, I think you're right. When he's seen the nurse, tell him to come to my office immediately," the boss said, still shaking his head.

Following the Christmas of '78 I received a letter, saying I'd been accepted to join the Civil Service in Sheffield working for the Inland Revenue. My bosses at British Steel were well pissed off at my decision to quit, but metallurgy wasn't for me. The lads I left behind were a great bunch, but it was a dirty environment, involved shift work, and held no interest.

On arriving at Sheffield 7 Tax Office, things couldn't have been more different. I was working in a plush office with a ratio of women to men 30 to 3. The two other chaps were both married, so the odds were definitely stacked in my favour. The work was tiresome and tedious, but the pay was okay, and it was warm. I was travelling back to Sheffield again, but this time it didn't feel so arduous.

After I'd been in the job two weeks, a friend of mine mentioned the possibility of working the holiday season in the Channel Islands. One phone call later, and I was set up for a job working as a bellboy at a hotel in St. Helier in Jersey, the largest of the Channel Islands. The job would commence that April, so first I had a three-month stint to work for the Revenue. During this period I got my head down and cracked on with the job in hand. Nothing of excitement happened whilst I was employed here, apart from the end-of-tax-year party. Jesus, it was a wild shindig. Booze a plenty and red-hot, frustrated women gagging for it. Being young, free and single I had a ball. It was like being in 'pass the parcel', with me being the parcel being passed from woman to woman. Their sexual appetites were insatiable, but I did my best for England. I wasn't in Burkie's league when it came to shagging thirty, but I did enough to make an impression.

Leaving the Revenue was sad, especially as I'd tapped off with a lady of twenty-nine, who taught me a thing or two in between the sheets. She would have won Olympic gold in bedroom gymnastics. She was funny as well as experienced, and I thoroughly enjoyed her company. But when I was saying my goodbyes to her, she simply brushed me aside like a piece of meat and told me she would see me around. I knew from day one that all this woman ever wanted from me was sexual gratification, but the way we parted, it angered and upset me. I'd been used and abused, and that wasn't going to happen again. I did, however, steal several pairs of her crotchless knickers, which I still parade around the house in to this day, when my wife's out shopping. I find doing the hoovering in them in very therapeutic.

I also wear a yellow ribbon tied in a bow on the end of my *todger*, but that's another story for my psychiatrist.

Jersey was everything and more than I'd expected it to be, and the beer was as cheap as chips. Four of us had made the journey over there; me and Salesy bagging posts prior to arriving there, and in the same hotel. The other two, Russ and Goober, found a nice little B&B run by two gays and to my knowledge, are still residing there as one big happy family, with Michael Barrymore visiting regularly, or so I'm led to believe. My place of work was called the Hotel Paraletico, accommodation specialising for young couples and swingers. The only swinging I knew about was on rope over Maltby beck, so this was a whole new ball game for me. My eyes were opened to a different world, one which took me quite by surprise.

My boss at the time was a gentleman called Egor, who had a wild beard and a glass eye. According to some of the lady reps who worked for the holiday company who owned the hotel, he was also a raving pervert. Being the bellboy, my job was to check customers in and carry their luggage to the rooms. It wasn't taxing or rocket science, but the tips were okay, and the customers were generally decent. The big perk with the job was some of the sights I witnessed and things I overheard from the bedrooms. You had to have an open mind to stay sane in my job, and I can remember Egor once saying to me,

"Alf, if you're too open minded your brains will fall out."

Egor had a wicked sense of humour, and like my Grandad, always had a joke or three up his sleeve. His wife Olga was a rotund woman with a ruddy face, always filling it with food of some kind. One morning, Egor and I were on reception checking the paper deliveries. Olga waddled past, still hung over from the night before, and still wearing the previous evening's dress. Apparently she had been to an all night party on the island with a few friends. She was munching a huge cheese butty the size of a dustbin lid. Egor tapped me on the shoulder and whispered in my ear,

"Alf, do you know the difference between single women and married women? Single women come home, look in the fridge and go to bed. Married women come home, look in the bed and go to the fridge."

I found Egor hugely entertaining; he was even better than Burkie. Women, however, found him repulsive. He was lecherous and creepy, and had a disgusting habit of sniffing the seat when a woman had vacated it. I'd seen my Grandad sniffing the milk to see if it was sour, but this was decidedly different. Egor liked to rub himself up against the female form at every opportunity. Olga realised his perversions, but chose to ignore them; she had another agenda, shagging the night porter. I tolerated Egor's behaviour because it didn't affect me. The thing that I most liked about him was his dry sense of humour. The guy was side-splittingly funny. He thought flatulence was a source of entertainment, a sort of self expression and male bonding. I couldn't fault him for this, and loved being party to his wise cracks.

On one particular afternoon, I was asked to help out the kitchen porter as the hotel was short staffed. Work was thin on the ground for me that day so I saw it as an opportunity to have some company. The kitchen porter wasn't the sharpest tool in the box, so when Egor came to lend a hand I was overjoyed. The 'KP' was slightly autistic and obsessive in his behaviour. Every pot, pan and plate was meticulously washed and dried and stacked away in exactly the right place. When I asked him why he was so fastidious, he said because Egor had told him he was 'judicious'. Was I hearing him right, did he just say judicious? I bet the 'KP' didn't understand the meaning of the word, so I pushed him further.

"What do you mean by 'judicious'?" I said.

The 'KP' looked up at me with his arms elbow-deep in water in the dirty sink water and replied,

"Hands that judicious are as soft as your face."

I turned to see Egor, who by now had his head inside the oven screaming with laughter.

Working with Egor was a blessing sometimes, as it alleviated the boredom of the long days stuck indoors when the sun was beating down outside. I once asked him how he had first met Olga. He explained to me that the pair of them had met at a cockles and mussels stall on Skegness sea front. Olga had inadvertently thrown pepper in Egor's direction causing him to sneeze violently. This nasal explosion triggered his glass eye to fly out, and miraculously Olga caught it in mid air. I asked him to elaborate on this, but all he said was,

"She happened to catch my eye."

Egor's all time classic quip was when one of the hotel guests complained about his gay partner's inappropriate actions. Apparently in a fit of rage, his partner had shoved a strawberry right up his arse. The man was obviously in discomfort, not to mention embarrassment. On listening to the man's anal predicament, Egor said,

"I've got some cream for that."

After working at 'Hotel Paraletico' for two months, I was fired for stealing strawberries. Not long afterwards, Egor and Olga split up; he finally caught her in the act of giving the night porter oral sex. Egor had been complaining that she had been conspicuous by her absence, and she ought to get her head down and get a proper job, the fat slut. She did, but the job in question was a blow-job!

Chapter 13
Mystic Aunt Louie

Perched on a hill overlooking Maltby is the tiny village of Hooton Levitt. Hooton, meaning 'farmstead on a spur of land' is mentioned in the Domesday Book, as Hoton or Hotune, which is derived from the Norse words *hoot*—hill, and *tun*—enclosed by a hedge. The Livet or Levett is an Anglo-Norman surname from the village of Livet-en-Ouche, Normandy, and was the manorial affix (estate) from the de Livet family that gained control of the manor in the 12th century after the marriage of Constance, granddaughter of Richard FitzTurgis, lord of the manors of Hooton and Wickersley, to William de Levet. The Levets disappeared during the reign of Henry V during a game of 'hide and seek', and were never seen again, or so it's said. I loved this little place, with its towering trees and excellent vantage point; you could see for miles across open farmland and pastures. It was also where my Aunt Louie and Uncle Alf lived.

Alf was an ex-farm worker who was small in stature but as strong as a bull. He smoked a pipe, which is somewhat of a rarity these days, and had a big purple bottom lip. The smell of his rough-shag tobacco filled the house, and I loved it. I never saw him without his beloved pipe; they were an item. Whenever he wanted to make me understand something, he always tapped me on the forehead with the bowl of his pipe. Another little trait of his was prodding me with the stem whenever he made a point about something, occasionally in the eye. He also wore an enormous leather pit belt around his gigantic waistline. He was a belligerent old bugger, grumpy as they come, opinionated and snappy to me, but I liked him all the more. With Alf, what you saw is what you got; he also shared the same forename as me which gave him leverage. Aunt Louie was totally the opposite. She was quiet, caring, affectionate, and special. She was a worrier and a deep thinker who possessed hidden talents; she could predict the future.

Aunt Louie's speciality was reading tea leaves. Tea leaf reading also known as tasseography or tasseomancy, has been practiced throughout the world for hundreds of years. It is the art of divination or fortune-telling that deciphers patterns in tea leaves. *Tasse* (French) or *tassa* (Arabic) means cup; and the Greek suffixes *graph*, and *mancy* mean study of or divination. It is thought that it has its origins in Asia and the Middle East, dating back as far as the sixth century. Tea didn't become popular in the West until the early 1600s.

Aunt Louie would only read your tea leaves if it felt right for her. Many a time she would refuse on the grounds that she didn't want to be the bearer of bad news for the recipient. If you were lucky enough and she decided to do you a reading, she'd pour your tea, without using a strainer, into a white china cup. When all the tea had been drunk—she hated waste—the cup would be shaken quickly and any remaining dregs would be swirled

round three times and the residue liquid carefully siphoned away. The cup was then placed in
an upright position, and she would stare intent-
ly into the bottom of it. After several minutes of
close examination of the patterns left by the tea
leaves she would disclose her predictions. Louie's
interpretations were frighteningly accurate, such
was her special gift. She never made a song and
dance about her psychic powers, and was a very
humble lady.

The shapes and patterns left by the tea leaves
in the base of the cup are analysed by the diviner
and translated accordingly. Louie would read the
cup from the present to the future by starting at
the rim of the handle and following the patterns
downwards in a circular manner until the bottom is reached; this symbolizes the distant future.
Symbols can be numerous things, from people to
inanimate objects. Louie told me that she used to
group nearby symbols together for a prediction. Her
method of interpretation was based on traditional
symbolism, passed on from generation to generation. If a symbol represented a candle, it would
mean enlightenment; a cat would be classed as a
deceitful relative or friend; an apple would signify
accomplishment; a raven would mean death.

Louie saw images only in dark tea leaves against
a white background. When she was actually studying the remnants of the leaves, she would take
on a different persona. Her face changed, and she
looked strangely distant. On some occasions when
I was witnessing her readings, I swear she looked
completely different, like someone else. I was

fascinated by her powers and asked her if she could teach me.

"Alas Alf I can't. You too have a special gift, but before you can realise your true potential and use this gift to your advantage you have to remove the curse that sits over your head," she said to me.

Well you can imagine how I felt, knowing some evil so-and-so had placed a curse over me. What was this curse, and how would it affect me? Louie said all would be revealed in good time. Patience has never been a strong point with me so this just sent my mind into overdrive; it also contributed massively to my out-of-control insomnia. I was now an owl by night and a zombie by day. It was at this stage in my life that I started to suffer from health anxieties and hypochondria. The next morning after I woke up and looked in the mirror, what I saw terrified me. I yanked Craig out of bed and said,

"Look at me. My hair's all matted and wiry, my skin's pimpled, my nostrils have grown, and my teeth are green."

Opening his gowl encrusted eyes, Craig stared at me and replied,

"Well there's nowt wrong with yer eyesight, Alf."

At this he turned over and went back to sleep. Grandad wasn't around anymore to ask his advice, so I went to visit Uncle Tony. I explained my predicament and told him what Aunt Louie had said about the curse and how she read tea leaves. Tony thought this a load of *balumcum*. He didn't believe in anything other than the power of his homemade grog. He ignored the curse element of my conversation and steered things around to the tea leaf readings. After I'd explained Aunt Louie's special gift, he sat me down and said,

"Look here Alf, I remember once going to the doctor's with excruciating piles. I'd been suffering from them for weeks. The doctor told me to drop my trousers, and on examining me said it was the worst case of *ceramics* he'd ever seen. He told me to go home and every night place a couple of damp tea bags on the haemorrhoids. I had to do this for two weeks. On returning to the surgery, I informed him that there'd been no improvement and could he tell me what to expect in the future. The doctor asked me to remove my trousers again, and part the cheeks of my arse for closer inspection. He stared intensely up my bum, and told me I would meet a tall dark stranger and go on a long journey."

After finishing his little story, Uncle Tony burst into a fit of laughter. I should have known better than asking his advice. Tony was a tormenting bugger at the best of times. Finding no answers at Tony's I sought advice further afield. Our local priest, Father Dew-Drop, was a man of wisdom. Even though he was new to the parish, I knew he'd see me and cast some light on things, hopefully easing my troubled mind. I raced over to the vestry and caught Father Dew-Drop sampling the communion wine. It was the middle of the afternoon, but Dew-Drop informed me in his slurred speech that this was the best time to sample wine; the temperature was just right. I had no reason to question or disbelieve him, so I ignored his drunken ramblings and explained my dilemma. In fairness to our new priest, he did seem interested in discussing my fears and concerns, but not at that particular moment. He said that he had a prior appointment with Mrs. Windsock, who had missed mass several times over the past month. He enlightened me to fact that he was going to put the fear of God up her behind the crypt. He arranged to meet me the following morning.

Still dressed in my previous day's garb, I shot out of bed, and scurried over to meet Father Dew-drop. On this occasion he was perfectly sober, and wearing a little smirk on his face. I ask him how his meeting had gone with Mrs. Windsock. Had he put the fear of God up her? He looked at me sheepishly and said,

"I gave her a sermon on the mount."

I hadn't a clue what he meant, so pressed on with my concerns over the curse. As I was chuntering on, Dew-Drop asked me to remove my flat cap as I was indoors, and this was deemed bad manners. I immediately apologised for my behaviour and explained that my Grandad had given it to me, and it was my treasured possession. He accepted my apology and took the cap from me, admiring the quality.

"I can see from the label inside the cap that it's very expensive and well made," he said.

"Sorry Father, but I've never looked inside the cap before. Grandad gave it to me a couple of years ago. You never knew my Grandfather did you?" I asked.

"I'm sorry to say I didn't young Alf. Did he used to have a wicked sense of humour?" the priest went on to ask.

I didn't understand where this line of questioning was leading to. I'd come to the church expecting to have the curse removed or even exorcised. Now he was cross examining me about my Grandad's sense of humour. What the hell was he on about? I looked at him square on and said,

"Why aren't you listening to what I'm saying to you about the curse? Shouldn't you be daubing me in holy water and dispelling demons from me or something?"

"Alf, calm down and listen to me. I'm not having a go at your Grandad. After reading this inscription inside your hat I feel that by removing it from your head will help remove the curse," Father Dew-Drop said, handing me the cap.

I stared into the lining and read the inscription out loud,

"If the cap fits, or so it's said, the wearer of this cap will have a shiny bald head. Something to look forward to in later life Alf. Love Grandad x."

Louie had obviously spotted this and was just teasing me. The curse hanging over my head was Grandad's little joke, it was as simple as that. All that fretting and worrying I'd put myself through was for nothing. Grandad still managed to have a laugh at my expense, even though he was dead, and thanks to the curse, I now have no hair...bastard!

Chapter 14
Perm any Mullet from Six

In the '70s, hairstyles took on a whole new dimension. It was the age of the hippies, and women opted for the more natural look, keeping their locks long, sleek and smooth. The time of sleeping with curlers in and having to endure endless hours of discomfort and pain because of the rolls and pin-up hairdos were finally over. No more did women have to look like poodles sporting ridiculous bouffants. The hippie movement with its free love and peace theme influenced trendy hairstyles in the '60s and '70s. Long straight hair parted in the middle was extremely popular, accentuated with ribbons or flowers.

Actress Farrah Fawcett of the American cult TV show 'Charlie's Angels' made a massive impact on chic hairstyles with her long 'winged' hair, and flicked back look. The famous model Twiggy chose a completely different image with her short-short hair, and for men, me included, by the end of the '70s the famous 'mullet' became all the rage; this was short in the front, and long at the back.

Back then, I never really worried about my hair; washing it every other week seemed sufficient enough as far as I was concerned, and split-ends gave it a natural, if greasy, flyaway look. I was blonde in my mid-teens with black facial hair sprouting through on my cheeks. It was fashionable to have

sideburns, or *sideboards* as we used to call, them
down the flanks of your mush. It was also trendy
to have a moustache, but mine resembled a football match (five-hairs-a-side), or a hairy caterpillar.
Even nowadays when I decide to grow a moustache,
I look like a cross between Rock Hudson when he
was dying with AIDS, poor soul, and a pervert. This
is a look I seldom opt for.

Young girls and boys loved the '70s. While
their parents were dealing with the three-day week,
raging strikes, rampant inflation, mass unemployment, and the Queen's Silver Jubilee, the youth
just kicked back and let all the world's problems
wash over them. The thing that really gripped the
nation was the *perm.* Around this time black power
and pride was emerging; this led to black men and
women allowing their usual tightly coiled hair to
grow out creating a huge mop or Afro.

The white population jumped on the band-
wagon and hairdressers up and down the country
were inundated with requests for perms. Our family managed to get all the kids and my mum done
in one sitting; mum secured a family discount for
the block booking. I'm sure if we would have asked
Pat at the hair salon, she would have given our dog
a *demi-wave* so he didn't feel too left out. Mum also
asked Pat if she could "black us up," such was her
love of the afro-style and her fascination with black
people and their music. On glancing at my brother,
Pat said she thought Craig was black enough. The
perm did suit a longer style of hair; mine however
was quite short so I resembled a *Brillo pad.* I never

really made it in the fashion stakes, not even when I boasted a good head of hair.

Along with Farrah Fawcett, other iconic TV personalities who carried off cool hairstyles were 'Starsky and Hutch', played by Paul Michael Glaser and David Soul. I tried to model myself on Hutch, who was blonde like me. Uncle Tony said I looked more like a rabbit hutch than an American detective. I never looked urbane or chic, more urban and shit.

When I visited Pat at the salon for my second perm, I was greeted by a young girl wearing a safety pin through her nose. I was somewhat shocked at this tribal look, but behind the metal was a wonderful girl with a lovely personality, according to Pat. She'd introduced music to the premises in the form of jazz/soul/funk, even though she professed to like all styles of popular music. To me she had the body of Baywatch and the face of Crime Watch. I wasn't interested; she actually intimidated me.

Her name was Christine, and she took great pains in telling me that she had two different coloured eyes, just like David Bowie; one green eye and one blue eye. What she neglected to mention was that they met in the middle and she was in fact cross-eyed. She flirted with me whilst fixing rollers in the womens' hair, before they sat under the dryers. Her blue and white striped pinafore was a stark contrast to the metal safety pin, and I couldn't help wondering what Pat was doing employing this anarchic-looking *sprog* in her shop. The other women paid no notice to her as their needles clattered together; knit one pearl one, cast off. You don't see women knitting any more. I was always fascinated how my mum could multitask by knitting, feeding the baby, ironing, cooking and getting the coal in all at the same time.

I once remember my mum going to the doctor and complaining that she couldn't get pregnant. The doctor examined her and said,

"Have you got the coil in?"

My mum looked at him disgruntled and replied,

"I haven't managed to finish washing the dishes yet, never mind getting coal in you cheeky bastard."

Getting back to the subject of hair, the beauty about having a perm was that you never had to comb it, or so I was led to believe. You just rinsed your head under the tap, shook it violently like a dog, and hey presto the curly look was achieved. Some guys did carry around large plastic Afro combs with them in their back pocket, but to me they just looked like dicks. It was brilliant having wavy hair; especially hair that didn't wave goodbye to your head like mine did at the age of twenty-five (thanks Grandad). I find it unbelievable nowadays those young guys with fantastic mops of hair are sweeping it forward, all in the name of fashion. I'd like to enlighten these youngsters by informing them there will be plenty of time for comb-overs when they get older.

When a perm starts to drop out, a *shaggy dog* look takes over. It starts to drop out from the top central part of the head and works its way outwards until it reaches the follicle extremities. After several weeks of a perm being done, when *drop out* is in full swing, you look like you are wearing a cowboy hat; round and smooth on top, curled up at the ends.

As the '70s neared its end, I was coerced into having a mullet cut by my mate Briels, who said it was all the fashion. Thirty years on and that bastard's still got his, along with a magnificent moustache. You probably think of me as bitter and twisted about losing my hair so young, whilst some of my so-called mates have retained theirs; you'd be right, I hate the fuckers. As previously mentioned, the mullet is a hair style that is short in the front and long in the back; it's also referred to as having "business in the front and party in the back".

The mullet is still around to this day and not just worn by Briels. It was classed as a rebellious hair style because of the length at the back which could be curly, straight or wavy. The mullet was usually accompanied by the wearer sporting a gold earring in their left ear. It was acceptable to prospective bosses and the likes because of its short and smart front section; the back could be tamed and controlled so as not to offend. It still is a hair style that basically says "I'm okay and responsible, but I have a tendency on a weekend to party and get wasted".

Whilst writing this book I asked numerous people about the origins of the mullet. Urban legend says Cornish fishermen wore their hair in this style to keep their backs warm. David Bowie helped raise the profile of the mullet, and years later Phil Collins tried desperately to recreate the style but didn't realise that the front section of the *barnet* had to be short, not bald. I also fell into this trap and looked equally pathetic. I have found numerous piss-taking web sites slagging the mullet off and naming and shaming people who choose to wear their hair in this style. Despite its reputation, the mullet is still popular in Argentina, Spain and Hellaby, Maltby's little village brother. In Spain it's associated with young gypsies and trouble-makers; in Argentina it's professional footballers, and in Hellaby it's simply sad fuckers who need to get a life (you know who I am referring to!).

A friend of mine once suggested that I should pursue a career in hairdressing. I always associated this profession with gay men, so maybe she was right—only joking all you gay people out there, I'm happily heterosexual, which is good news for all of you. I would have made a rubbish hairdresser and an even worse gay. They say "don't knock it until you've tried it." Well I did once, and never again. It's not big and it's not clever.

I was fortunate to go to school with several hairdressers who have all made fantastic livings from their careers. They are all equally multi-talented and cool, and were all pretty gifted with their fists. This came in handy for one particular mate who did happen to be homosexual. Duncan was harassed and persecuted at his salon in Wakefield, and had to dish out some of his own chastisement to a couple of macho guys who were giving him grief. They daubed excrement on the door handle of his premises, sent him and his partner hate mail, and outed him about his alleged homosexuality in the local newspaper. He did get his revenge one evening, when he kidnapped the pair of them from the Poacher's Hole public house and took them both on a joy ride; which was indeed a very gay outing. He used his fists on and in the pair of them, and sorted the differences they had out there and then. The *fist-crippler* had the desired effect, and both these gentlemen are now regulars at the Wakefield salon, the new gay bar 'The Crumb-Sucker', and Michael Barrymore concerts.

Looking back at old photographs from this era, my two kids scream with laughter at my bad hair styles. My only consolation is that everyone used to have the same hideous mops. Even back then we were all victims of fashion. They say "fashion is fleeting but style lasts forever." My hair, like fashion was definitely fleeting. As far as style goes, I've never really been blessed with any, so I wouldn't know what I was missing. Whatever people still say about the mullet, and however much this iconic hair style is ridiculed, I'd give my left kidney to sport a Spanish mullet any day of the week.

Chapter 15
Newquay Nights

One eventful week that springs to mind from my mid-teens was a calamitous holiday me and the boys had in Newquay. The brochure described it as "the coast of dreams," offering a rare mix of wonderful coastline, spectacular beaches washed clean by the Atlantic Ocean, soaring cliffs and brilliant surfing. What a load of shite; it was more like the "Blackpool of the West Country." Back in the late '70s getting down to the south-western section of Great Britain was both tedious and long.

The coach trip to Cornwall and back took up nearly half your vacation. We set off at midnight on Friday after a session in the Swan; five of us travelled by charabanc, whilst two other reprobates went by car. In reality the journey did in fact take nine hours, with only one toilet break. I think the tour operator expected that all the passengers would drop off to sleep as it was a night passage; not a prayer. We wanted to party all the way, much to the annoyance of the rest of the holiday makers. Laden down with wine and Pro-Plus tablets, we headed straight for the back seat of the bus. We hadn't even got out of the pub car park before the driver stopped the coach and stormed down the aisle towards us.

"If you *effing* idiots don't cut it out and calm

down you'll be off this vehicle before we reach Hellaby!" he ranted.

We acknowledged his request by doing a *Moonie* and yelling at him, "Bollocks!"

As he pulled out of Low Road, instead of turning left towards the motorway, he turned right and drove straight to the police station some five hundred yards away; we'd only been on the bus two minutes, and before I could even adjust my underpants we were being cautioned by the police. It had the desired effect and we quietened down, to the relief of everyone on board. That was until we had got forty miles or so down the M1, then the *beano* kicked off again. I had secretly dressed up as the 'Incredible Hulk' and painted my face green, complete with ebony wig. I sported a lime green ripped shirt and black torn half-master trousers with no shoes or socks. I raced down the aisle of the coach screaming like a banshee at my fellow passengers pretending to be the 'Hulk', (played by the gargantuan Lou Ferrigno). I scared everyone shitless, including some old aged pensioners just dozing off to sleep. The driver slammed his anchors on and pulled over onto the hard shoulder of the motorway.

"What the bleeding hell do you think you're doing lad?" he snapped.

"Don't make me angry. You wouldn't like me when I'm angry," I growled back at him, still in character.

The accidental dose of gamma radiation mixed with Bull's Blood had interacted with my brain cells and started my metamorphosis into the 'Hulk'. Well, that's what I told the Nottingham Police when they boarded the bus and arrested me. After some grovelling and crocodile tears the East Midland Constabulary allowed me back onto the bus, much to everyone's displeasure, including some of my mates. I laughed it off like the obnoxious twat I was back then and carried on pricking around. That was until a large chap from Bramley walked straight up to me and smashed his fist into my face; I immediately sat down and never muffed another word for the remainder of the journey—due to my jaw being dislocated.

Our arrival in Newquay was a lot more sedate than the departure from Maltby. Our buddies in the car had been waiting for us for two hours; they had already booked into a plush hotel on the seafront. On checking directions to our squat we suddenly realised that it was two miles out of town, and taxis back then cost us an arm and a leg so it was *Shank's pony* for us lot. Just short of one hour later we finally reached our destination, which turned out to be a dilapidated farmhouse in the middle of nowhere. Having checked in I was delighted to find a television in the main sitting room. Still feeling groggy from the blow to the jaw, I decided to stay put for a few hours to recuperate.

The telly was black and white, but at least it took my mind off the pain I was enduring. All the other lads quickly changed and made their way off to the beach, as it was a beautiful sunny day. Slumped in a rickety chair my 'one-eyed get off my land' Cornish host kindly gave me a mug of cider to quell the suffering a little; it kind of did the trick I must admit. Back then there were only three TV channels; BBCI, BBC2 and a local ITV channel, depending on which region you were in. Everyone therefore saw the same programmes, like *The Generation Game, Porridge, Morecombe and Wise*. These greats have still to this day stood up to the test of time. Morecombe and Wise got over thirty million viewers, which seems incredible in today's multi-channel world. Peer group pressure to watch popular shows was immense, so you could have a conversation about them the next day with your buddies and work colleagues without feeling left out.

I must have dropped off for an hour or so and when I realigned my jaw I decided to get changed and make my way into Newquay to meet up with the lads. I eventually stumbled upon them on Fistral Beach, a huge sandy expanse which is one of the best surfing beaches in the UK, and has the best beach breaks in Cornwall: Unfortunately, they were being chased by an old guy waving his walking stick at them. Apparently they had dropped back into the childish mode and had been soaking holiday makers through with water pistols, pretending to be the stalwart Steve McGarrett of 'Hawaii Five-O'. I distinctly heard Smig shout, "Book 'em Danno!" prior to unleashing his water cannon on a cluster of unsuspecting sunbathers. Smig had the tousled, yet immovable hairstyle of Jack Lord back then; now he looks more like Harry Hill.

That evening me and the guys decided to go clubbing at 'Tall Trees' night club. We had no idea how to dress to impress. There was a time when I wore flares, polyester shirts and platforms. When you're young you can blame sartorial faux pas on the folly of age. I still wear these types of clothes now; so what's my excuse, I hear you say. The simple answer is that I don't give a hoot any more. So long as I'm comfortable and can get the zip of my yellow and purple striped cords down quickly for the loo, I'm happy, even though my kids say I look as cheesy as *fook*.

To atone for my error of judgement in the fashion stakes I wore several ear rings to deflect from my attire. It seemed to do the trick somewhat and I never really had a problem bagging a slag or two at the end of the evening when they were verging on falling into a coma through drink; come to that, neither did the rest of the lads. My heinous crime with style was further complicated by my lack of dancing skills; I was pathetic. Thank God Chalkey was around as I had a slight edge on him. He was dreadful, and still is. Chalkey's claim to fame was his quick acerbic wit. Whilst smooching with a lady somewhat older than him on the dance floor to The Commodores classic 'Three Times a Lady' Chalkey was heard to say to his dance partner,

"You're once, twice, three times my age."

She stormed out of the disco, crying her eyes out. We all fell about laughing our respective tits off. Chalkey was a bit of a bastard like that, but a funny bastard I have to say; he's nearly as funny as me, but that's another story.

Staggering out of the club, we all headed off for a hamburger or three to soak up the beer. Unfortunately for Chalkey, he wandered off elsewhere and was subsequently leathered by the husband of the woman he'd ridiculed about her age. I remember him reeling like a pin-ball from one side of the street to the other, blood splattered down his three-piece cream suit with matching brown kipper tie. He looked dreadful; we ended up supporting him back to the B&B. His normal haughtiness and smug smile that he wore all day from getting up in the morning was nowhere to be seen; it had been replaced by something resembling a wide-mouthed frog, complete with dried blood and snot.

The following morning we hit the beach again, only this time minus the water cannons. As fate would have it we pitched up alongside two stunning Swedish girls. They had bright blue eyes, golden-brown skin, legs right up to their necks and breasts worth saluting. We started trying to impress them by doing hand-stands and play-fighting with each other, all to no avail. Smig suggested that we had a go at body-boarding. What a complete disaster this turned out to be. I scraped all the skin off my chest along the shingle beach which I'm sure was blended with razor blades. Smig sprained his ankle and Chalkey bust his nose again turning the sea red; with Newquay's reputation for shark sightings, the water was cleared quicker than in the 'Jaws' movie.

As we hobbled back to our towels the Swedish nymphets started to giggle at us like little school girls.

"What's so funny girls?" Chalkey asked, breathing in and puffing his chest out at the same time.

"It's you guys. You're all so small," one of them replied.

Immediately we all glanced down at our respective willies. Yes the sea water was freezing, and yes we didn't fill out our *Speedo* trunks like David Beckham; in fact, if truth be known, one inch smaller and we would have all been girls. We tried to laugh it off but when the size of a bloke's *todger* comes in for questioning, they retreat back into their own small worlds.

"Well at least mine's filled a pram twice," Russ chipped in.

"No we don't mean the size of your penis; we mean your height in general," the same girl replied.

Thank God for that, we all murmured to each other. It was at this stage of the conversation that Chalkey stuffed two large pebbles down my trunks, giving the impression of my gonads resembling a cross between a small bag of spuds and the Elephant Man. Cockily I placed my hands on my hips and pushed my chest out like a peacock; if this didn't impress them, nothing would. As luck would have it, one of the pebbles made a break for it and leapt out of my trunks and onto my foot. Game over.

I'd been in Newquay only a few days and had suffered a dislocated jaw and broken big toe. The rest of my vacation was spent sunbathing quietly on my own; I did get a wonderful tan, although my foot was as white as Marley's ghost. My only consolation was that Heidi, one of the Swedes, felt sorry for me and gave me a blow-job and a power-wank on the last night. Now who's laughing boys?

Chapter 16
A Pain through the Window

In between proper jobs, having returned from Jersey, I got temporary employment at a window and door manufacturing firm in Hellaby, working as a warehouse operative. It was the summer holidays and life felt good for a change; even though it was menial work and bored me senseless. I was given the opportunity to drive a three-tonne lorry, delivering the merchandise along the east coast of England.

When you're seventeen and have only just passed your driving test three weeks earlier, the chance to get behind the wheel of a 'juggernaut' (*slight* exaggeration) makes a lad feel a million dollars. I suddenly became the 'Yorkie' man, such was my desire to be a lorry driver. When I started to learn to drive, the lessons were only £2.50 per hour, which to me was a fortune. I managed to have six lessons over a twelve-month period, and passed first time, much to the astonishment of my driving instructor who thought I was useless. I proved her wrong and suddenly had the freedom of the road; the highways and byways became my new playground in the company's vehicle.

The only downside to being out on the road in the big van was that my specific driving day was

Thursdays; the rest of the working week was spent in the warehouse stacking windows and doors and sweeping up. Being blessed with the accursed hay fever during the summer months, the dust from the floor gave me dreadful sneezing fits, to the extent that I struggled to breathe. I quickly worked a deal with my fellow employees that I would unload all the lorries that came into the depot and stack the goods, and they would keep the warehouse dust-free. My fellow workers were somewhat older than me so they felt that this was an excellent compromise, and everyone was happy.

My immediate boss was a guy called Colin Harvester, and I must say that he was the original 'mad professor'. The man was deranged, both in looks and temperament. He had wild hair, was missing his top two front teeth, and had a huge cyst on the top of his head. I loved working with him because of his irrational behaviour. I'd been brought up with Uncle Noggin, so to me, this was normal everyday life. He used to have a nasty habit of spitting when talking, and people would say to him, "Say it don't spray it." The spittle would fly from his mouth like tracer bullets, making you duck for cover, for fear of losing an eye.

He also walked at great speed, darting across the warehouse like a pin-ball, banging against the stacks of doors and windows. Everything he did was at a fast and furious pace, resulting in him causing numerous accidents both to himself and others. He was permanently agitated and wound up, and would storm off in a huff at the slightest little thing, waving his arms frantically in the air, shouting at the top of his voice.

The first time I witnessed his bizarre and dangerous behaviour was early one morning when several of us were loading the lorry prior to a delivery later that day. We happened to be lifting heavy fire-doors onto the back of the vehicle. Our guy on the lorry was a chap called Astrix, who was in his late eighties and extremely lackadaisical and slow.

The office doors flew open and Colin raced down the aisle to where we happened to be working, screaming to us that we'd better get a move on or we be sacked for failing to get the order out on time. Observing the fact that we had only loaded six doors onto the wagon, he immediately elected himself chief loader, and snatched a door from me. I must stress that fire-doors are cumbersome and weighty, need care when lifting, especially when hoisting them a metre off the ground.

"Give me that door you idle oaf. We haven't got all day. Get out of my way and let me show you how to load this bloody vehicle quickly and efficiently," he yelled into my lug-hole.

Colin shoved me to the ground in a fit of rage and grabbed the door from me, hurtling it upwards onto the rear of the lorry. Without waiting to see if Astrix had secured it, he turned to me and said,

"That's how to load a door quickly Alf. Look and learn boy."

I was still on the floor dusting myself down whilst simultaneously sneezing. I peered up and suddenly realised Astrix hadn't actually caught hold of Colin's door. Colin was stood with his back to the lorry, and the door was falling towards him. Before I could alert him to the impending danger, the door *twatted* him straight over the top of his head, rendering him unconscious. His glasses shot forward and hit me in the groin; he was now underneath the fire-door.

Me and the chaps wrenched the door off him and noticed the egg on his head had burst, with blood gushing out like a tap. Whenever I get into circumstances like this I tend to get the giggles; I know I sound shallow and uncaring, but this couldn't be further from the truth. I just can't help myself; the more I try to quell the guffaw, the worse it becomes, making me look evil and sick. On this occasion I didn't need to feel any pangs of guilt, as all the other blokes began pissing themselves with laughter. Poor old Colin was *sparko*, and we were all stood around howling at the man's misfortune.

Another event springs to mind with regards to working with Colin. One sunny afternoon, two big low-loaders entered the depot at the same time. My colleagues realised I wouldn't be able to shift such a huge volume of windows by myself, so reluctantly agreed to help. Colin clocked the vehicles and made himself conspicuous by his absence, hidden in the cabin on the mezzanine floor with his special magazines. I didn't mind the physical humping and told the chaps to leave it to me. It would take me a little longer than usual, but the drivers informed me that they weren't in a hurry. I got stuck in and within the hour had the cargo unloaded and stacked neatly away.

As if by magic Colin appeared and informed me that I'd stacked the merchandise the wrong way round. Now the pile of windows was almost eight feet high consisting of at least twenty large frames, and the weight of each casement was considerable. I could see no point in arguing so I decided to restack the whole lot again as per Colin's instructions, only this time I would add my own special touch to the proceedings.

Having got almost all the frames restacked, I took off my rubber safety gloves and boots and filled them with toilet paper to pad them out. Five frames up from the bottom of the stack I wedged the boots under two frames so they were sticking out. Several feet up from this I did the same with my gloves. To all intents and purposes it gave the outward appearance that someone was stuck inside the stack, and had trapped their hands and feet. I know it sounds absurd and ridiculous, but you have to take into consideration the person I was dealing with at the time: the village idiot! When I'd got everything in place, I notified the blokes about my intentions and we all hid around the corner, waiting to monitor Colin's reactions. I deliberately toppled over two frames to give the desired effect of an accident, and screamed out for Colin's assistance. On hearing my fake cries, Colin motored down to the scene of the calamity, and shouted,

"Don't worry Alfie-Boy, I'll save you. Oh and don't move in case you've broken anything."

I sniggered quietly about his last remark, not trying to move in case I broke anything. With a shed-load of windows supposedly on top of me, I was hardly going to be in a position to move freely. Colin clambered up the stack and started hurling the timber casements off the pile like a man possessed. Broken and damaged frames littered the warehouse floor, and throughout his frantic efforts he was reassuring me that he would save me. When he finally arrived at the section where my gloves were popping out, and realised I wasn't there, his first reaction was one of desperation.

"Alf, where is your head and body?" he said looking all perplexed and concerned.

"It's right here Colin," I replied, appearing from behind another stack of windows.

The look on his face was priceless. It was a cross between being delighted that I wasn't dead and totally pissed off that he'd been made to look such a fool. I was instantly sacked on the spot, for my tomfoolery and shenanigans.

The following day I was reinstated at the behest of my fellow workers, on the grounds that I was such a good grafter. As you can imagine, Colin was mega hacked off with me and swore revenge. Bring it on I thought; there's nothing better than a minor war between two adversaries. That same afternoon, I was asked to deliver two doors to a building site in nearby Wickersley. As the load was so small, I used the owner's estate car for my transport. Whenever we conveyed doors on the roof rack of a car, we always ensured that we placed cover-doors underneath and on top of our cargo for protection. A cover-door was usually an old or reject door we had laying about the yard. The delivery went to plan, the site foreman slipped me a quid for my troubles and off I went. With a pound in my *sky-rocket*, the only thoughts I had in my miniscule brain at the time were ones of spending it that night on a few pints of beer. I'd forgotten about fastening the two cover-doors down on the roof rack.

As I zoomed down the dual carriageway back to work, the wind caught hold of my unsecured doors and whisked them high up into the stratosphere. They must have ascended thirty feet or so before they began their clumsy descent to the ground. I watched all this happen through my rear view mirror, never thinking that they were my doors. In seconds they had smashed into an oncoming milk float, emptying its entire contents all over the carriageway. Meanwhile, I was well down the road, arse twitching like Bill Oddie's eye, thinking, "I hope nobody thinks that it had anything to do with me". On this occasion I was lucky; not so the following day.

Driving home in the passenger seat of Colin's 'Skoda Automobile', as he used to refer to it, we happened to get stuck in a queue of traffic at a busy junction in Hellaby. It was rush hour so there was nothing we could do other than sit patiently in the traffic. Colin had other ideas. His protestations could be heard for miles. He was gripping the steering wheel and rocking forwards and backwards, like a deranged baboon that had been caged all its life.

"Why aren't we bloody moving? What's the chuffing problem? What's the bleeding world coming to? I've a good mind to write to my MP demanding he sorts the state of this junction out. Does he not realise my tea will be cold when I eventually get home, the imbecile," Colin ranted.

I turned my head towards the back seat to acknowledge my mate Roy's pat on my shoulder. He winked and made a secret hand gesture to me, and I instantly knew what he intended me to do. Between the pair of us we had carried out this manoeuvre several times on unsuspecting victims whilst being passengers in a car. With a quick nod from my buddy in the back, I lent sideways and threaded my right hand through Colin's arms. Meanwhile, my mate had lurched forward and clasped his arms around Colin's waist trapping his arms in the process. Colin now was unable to move.

My right hand carefully meandered its way up towards the front windscreen and formed a 'V' shape; it's also referred to as giving someone the 'forks', 'flagging off', 'giving the bird', or basically indicating to someone to *fuck off!* Simultaneously I held my left hand on the car horn ensuring I attracted the attention of the driver in the car in front of us. Colin was wriggling like an eel trying desperately to struggle free, but to no avail, thanks to Roy's strong and tight grip. With the deafening noise of the horn, and the unwelcome hand signals from Colin, it didn't take the driver in front too long before he had leapt out of his vehicle and was hammering his fists on top of Colin's roof.

"Who the hell do you think you are pal?" he bellowed.

Roy had now lessened his grip on Colin and I had removed my offending hands from the window and off the car horn. Colin jumped out of the car protesting his innocence, but the bloke was having none of it. Then God pressed the remote to pause and everything stopped. The guy from the other car peered into our vehicle through my opened passenger window and looked directly at me and said, "Aren't you that idiot from yesterday who caused my milk float to overturn in Wickersley because of your flying doors?"

Before I had time to pass the buck and blame someone else, he reached in and punched me straight in the face. I vaguely remember Roy saying something along the lines of "Now who's the pain through the window?"

Chapter 17
An Unwelcome
Birthday Present

Over the Christmas period coming up to my eighteenth birthday, me and a few mates had got drunk and were dicking around, up to mischief and playing pranks on people. I cannot divulge the trouble we caused as the police in Maltby have never closed the file, so the investigation is still live. Needless to say it was bad, to the extent that at ten past nine on the morning of my birthday I was arrested and taken down to the Police Station on High Street in Maltby. Kids nowadays aren't afraid of the police anymore and see them more of a nuisance than the actual law of the land. I regularly witness kids as young as five spitting at police men and telling them where to get off, but enough about my nephews.

When the police arrived at our house that cold morning, I was reluctant to get out of my bed, until they assisted me by grabbing my hair and yanking me across the bedroom floor. It certainly had the desired effect, and I was wide awake in milliseconds. On that particular occasion there were two police officers present; one male and one female. I laugh when I think of it now, because the only thing I was wearing at the time was a pair of blue lace girls' knickers—well I was into Rod Stewart in the '70s, and he reckoned it was sexy, and that was good enough for me. What a complete twat I must have looked. Thank God, like most young men in a morning, I was in a state of semi-arousal, so I amply filled my small underwear, which was excellent as it was the female officer who handcuffed me.

I pretended not to care and act the big man, whilst protesting my innocence saying, "You'll never take me alive," and "I'm too young to be raped in a cell," all to no effect. The officers attending just roughly escorted me down the stairs into a waiting police car. They did allow me to get dressed, which was relatively difficult with my hands being behind my back in handcuffs, however logic prevailed and I was let loose for a few minutes to properly attire myself. Down at the nick I was taken in to meet the custody sergeant and had my finger prints taken. I remember the officer in charge asking me to relax my wrist, otherwise he would break it. I was then whisked off to an interview room where I was questioned about a crime I'd supposedly been involved in.

I opted to stick to the criminal's code of conduct and said bugger all. I started to act cocky at one stage, but the female officer in attendance slapped me so hard across the face I was only able to masticate my food sideways like a sheep for the following week.

I feel sorry for coppers now as they are just political puppets for the left-handed liberal do-gooders. Police should be allowed to patrol the streets in numbers, and the United Kingdom should adopt the 'Broken Window Policy' with zero tolerance on even petty crime. Now don't get me wrong, back in the late '70s and early '80s I went off the rails, and caused myself and others around me a lot of trouble. I was mixed up and challenged society and its rules, but fundamentally I was still afraid of the boys in blue, and as much as I hated them, I did respect them. When you come to think about it, just because the police have a few bad apples in their ranks, which seem to spoil their otherwise spotless image, we as a nation shouldn't be too hard on them.

I recently telephoned the police to report a burglary on my street, and ended up arguing with a pre-recorded message. When the police arrived three years later to investigate the crime, my neighbour had died—well his wife had murdered him for granny porn—and I couldn't remember what the burglar looked like. They gave me such a hard going over for wasting their valuable time, and severely scolded me for having a bald head in a detached house, which does seem fair on reflection.

Whenever I talk to anyone about current crime sprees, including knife crime, drive-by shootings, drug pushing, murder and litter dropping, I always get the same response from my audience; more police on the streets. The fact that we have 'no-go' areas in inner city suburbs is ludicrous. Mob rule is a thing that happened in Roman times, not nowadays. The police, and the army for that matter, should take the streets back under proper control. I blame two specific groups for law and disorder; the Government and the parents. They say that we deserve the government we elect.

Wrong; proportional representation would sort this out fairly and squarely. With regards to parents and their offspring, when a kid commits a crime, hit them where it hurts, in their pockets.

I read in the newspapers that the prisons are full to capacity; that indicates to me that as a nation we have become soft on crime, and prisons are now like hotels. Bollocks to human rights, an eye for an eye, that's what I say. All the migrants that have drifted into this country for an easy ride should be made to work and contribute to society in general, including keeping money in this country and paying taxes here. Get the unemployable to help the less fortunate, old aged pensioners and the likes; they always need their gardens cutting, their shopping delivered, incontinence bags changing and someone to listen to their constant whinging and moaning.

After several hours inside a police cell, the female officer who had kindly rearranged my face whisked me off to another interview room; the previous one I'd been in was now occupied by my mate Briels. He was also being interrogated, both verbally and with an anal probe. I knew that Briels wouldn't spill the beans—knowing him like I did I knew that he wouldn't part with the steam off his shit—so like him I kept my gob firmly shut.

"Your mate in the next room has confessed to everything. He said that you are the main culprit; it was your idea and you held the match," the officer said to me.

"Match, what match?" I replied.

"Ah, you admit there was a match involved. Come on lad; confess the lot and we'll see if we can get you only ten years in prison, as opposed to life," was the officer's retort.

Ten years as opposed to life. What the heck were they on about? Our mini crime spree was good but it didn't warrant anything more than a hefty fine.

"Are you sure you haven't got me mixed up with someone else, like Idi Amin or Pol Pot?" I protested.

"Shut up bollock-brains. We ask the questions here not you. Now admit it, you started the fire," she went on.

I now realised that they had got the wrong guy, so in my infinite wisdom decided to string things along for a while. They had started this game, so I might as well join in. Stood directly behind the female constable was a big, burly copper who looked like a bull dog. He remained silent but gave off a menacing air. His body odour was also rancid. I peered up and looked directly into his eyes, which seemed to antagonise him somewhat. The female bobby resumed her bizarre line of questioning.

"Who supplied the matches then?"

Here we go again, I thought. She's obviously a secret twisted fire-starter or underground arsonist. Why did she keep pushing the match theory? But I didn't want to sound too inquisitive and ask any more questions, for fear of getting another good hiding. What with the bulldog in the background I thought my best line of defence would be to say nowt. This seemed to piss her off even more than answering her back. She doled out another crack, which connected on my ear, and I yelped in pain.

"I'll ask you one more time, then it's the probe, and you don't know where that's been," the constable said.

I did, but I thought about keeping this vital information to myself. Me and Briels had shared bodily fluids before so this didn't worry me too much. Before you all start jumping to conclusions, we were *blood brothers*; (something friends can't do anymore for fear of AIDS. Briels never caught AIDS until his mid-twenties so I was safe then). With the whack to the lug-hole, for some strange reason it made me sneeze.

I sneezed so loudly it frightened the butch guy and his female accomplice, to the extent that they stepped backwards and knocked the interview table over, causing such a racket that it alerted the custody sergeant who entered the room. Due to my violent nasal explosion, my face and shirt were now covered in blood. The sergeant's reaction was one of panic; he obviously thought his comrades had gone too far with the torture process trying to get me to confess. Realising this and to stoke the fire up (keeping on the matches and arson theme) I began sobbing for England.

The female copper started to panic and pretended to console me. I fell to the floor and clung to her knees begging her not to hit me anymore. It was pandemonium. The sergeant went ape-shit at the pair of them and seemed genuinely concerned about my health and welfare. He grabbed the pair of them by the epaulettes and flung them out of the room. Picking up a nearby tea-towel he handed it to me and asked me to try to stem the blood. At this stage of proceedings I pretended to faint, and fell to the floor with the grace of Didier Drogba. The sergeant pressed an alarm button and before you could strike another match, the room was full of coppers trying desperately to assist me. Five minutes earlier two of their colleagues had been trying to knock my brains out. What a turnaround this had become. Suddenly I was the victim and the police were the culprits.

After a lot of red faces and apologies I was released without charge. The time was 2.40 pm and the White Swan public house would be calling last orders at 3.00 pm. From the police station to the pub was a good five minutes, so I set off like the wind, running so fast that I arrived two minutes before I set off. Craig had eight pints lined up on the bar for me. My mates, thinking me still locked up, were hovering around like vultures, waiting for the chance to strike and pounce. I steamed into the lounge bar and sank the first pint in one. *It slaked the dust*, as my Uncle Jack used to say. I got a spontane-ous round of applause from my mates, who I think were pissed off that I'd turned up and stopped them pilfering the ale. One minute later, Briels burst in and started quaffing one of my allotted pints. He also finished it in one gulp, then looked at me and winked.

"You didn't tell 'em anything Alf. Did you?" he said.

"Of course not you dozy pillock. Drink up and I'll tell you what that entire rumpus was about in the room I was in," I replied.

I managed to drink four pints that afternoon, before time at the bar was called; Briels helped me with the rest.

All my mates loathed the police. When I come to think about it, they never really did anything specific to piss us off; after all, it was us that caused the grief, and they just did the mopping up. During the week of my birthday, the police attended our house five times, which is still my all-time record. All I got was the odd thump in the mouth and scuff around the ear. I wasn't charged, which was down more to luck than judgement. My mum was angered that all our neighbours thought Ronnie Biggs had moved in, but I was relatively unfazed by the limelight.

One good thing came out of my brushes with the law; girls love a bad boy. My reputation soared to great heights—well it was at rock bottom, so it did have far to climb—and I was inundated with girls asking me out. I played up to the part of a villain—like Burt Lancaster who starred in the epic film 'The Birdman of Alcatraz'—only I was more like the 'Sparrow of Maltby'. I pretended that I'd battled with the police inside the station, and had knocked three of them out before they managed to shackle me in the electric chair, which of course I had escaped from. There was no end to my fantasising, but the girls loved it. I went on to become Maltby's answer to 'Citizen Smith' and started to think of myself as a revolutionary.

The original *Citizen Smith* starred Robert Lindsay as 'Wolfie' Smith, a young urban Marxist guerrilla whose catch-phrase was "Power to the People," The show was a British television sitcom which ran from 1977 through to 1980. Wolfie was the self-proclaimed leader of the Tooting Popular Front, and I became the head of the infamous 'Cliff Hills Mafia'. My left-wing ideals were a joke and ill-thought out. I'd no idea what the hell I was supposed to be or what I was representing, but back then it didn't seem to matter. What was important was that all the young fillies around me loved the idea of a *Che Guevara* figure in their midst. *El Che*, as he was also known, believed from his early travels through Latin America, that the devastating and endemic poverty he witnessed was mainly due to the deep rooted economic inequalities, attributed to the constitutional result of monopoly imperialism and capitalism.

I was known as *El Sie* (named after a friend's aunt) and from my early travels through the deprived Model Village and White City areas of Maltby, realised that all the poverty I witnessed was due to the fact that the inhabitants were working class, simple as that. All inequalities in relation to poverty are a result of the capitalist upper classes exploiting the lower working classes. In Maltby we just accepted this as a way of life; ignorance is bliss. Being working class and poor went hand in hand. The masses never questioned the master.

To this day I still don't understand the disparity between what is right and fair. We live in a society where greed and avarice is king, and the welfare of mankind is not worth bothering about. Without meaning to name-drop, the other day I had lunch with Donald Trump at the Ivy in Rotherham, and we both agreed over a bottle of Dom Perignon that poor people should occasionally be allowed to eat asparagus; if you think long and hard about it, I think you will agree!

I would like to end this chapter by stating quite categorically that I have no real political beliefs or ambitions, am not an ardent criminal, was never referred to as *El Sie,* and have never met Donald trump in Rotherham. For the record, I met him in New York at the 'Conservative Cat Burglars and Fire Starters' Conference'—for the over forties whose surname begins with 'E'. So there you have it in a nutshell. You shouldn't try to be what you are not. Be yourself and live life to the full. If you happen to be filthy rich, that's not your fault. Just be mindful to contribute to charity, and remember, charity begins at home.

Chapter 18
Friday Night,
Saturday Morning

After working a full week, come six o'clock on Friday night I was ready to party. Having arrived home at half past five I would quickly shower and brush my teeth, then it was out with the boys. Briels was normally waiting at our front door, such was his thirst for beer and women. Having reached the Brooklands Club, we would order several pints of *rocket-fuel* lager and the night was off and running. Working men's clubs were magnificent in the '70s and '80s. Downstairs in the Brooklands we had a full size snooker table, darts board, a one-armed bandit that paid out £100 jackpots, great camaraderie, and a total set of wankers, more commonly known as 'the Committee'.

Darts and dominoes were very popular sports in pubs and clubs throughout the UK in the late '70s, and severely contested by all who participated. I've witnessed many a fight because someone has accused a fellow player of cheating, especially when competing at dominoes. 'Five and Threes', and 'Corners' or 'Windmill' as it was sometimes known, were the games played a lot back then, and I loved to observe the older guys pretending to study their hand whilst simultaneously studying their partner's hand as it was far more interesting. My late Grandad was a domino champion, along with his mates Charlie Potter and Cheddar. He taught me the trick of always playing dominoes with a mirror in the close vicinity, angled right to see your opponent's hand. You'd be surprised how many people fell for this simple trick, such was their enthusiasm to play the game. Darts on the other hand, was acute vision and skill.

Every Friday evening around seven a group of the lads would get together and play either 'Killer' or 'Shanghai'. In Killer a player owns a number on the dartboard and competes with other players to build up lives by hitting that particular number three times. When the threshold has been reached, the player attempts to kill his/her opponents by removing the lives they have built up, by hitting the other player's specific numbers. I loved Killer with a passion. Shanghai, on the other hand is a game where you start on one and work your way around to seven. The object of the game was to hit the treble, double and single with just three darts. Points are allocated during the game, and on reaching seven, all the points are added up; the winner is the one with most points. I wasn't too bothered about this game, as I always lost.

About twelve of us would play Killer, and each player would throw a pound into a kitty; winner takes all. On numerous occasions I was down to the last two with all my lives intact, whilst my opponent was down to his last life. I could smell the money, it was so close; and then Wack Walker would enter the room. He would scrutinise the score board and realising I was about to make off with the pot of cash, snarl at my opponent, who would immediately hand over his darts to him, due to fear of imminent death. Wack would then throw the darts anywhere, including at various people who happened to be standing around spectating; he didn't really understand or care about the rules of the game. I would pretend to think this act of grown-up bullying was fine, and occasionally join in and throw my darts at passers-by; this usually meant at Chalkey.

The game was as good as over, and Wack would collect the pot, split it 80/20 in his favour and wink at me. He was a big bloke, but underneath his gargantuan frame was a cheeky bugger who got away with murder. Later at the bar, he'd split it down the middle with me, telling me that on examining the odds when he arrived he felt I was going to lose, so half the money was better than none. Due to his magnificent gladiatorial physique and the fact that he had hands like shovels, I always concurred with his logic and reasoning. I still see Wack occasionally in Maltby. He is still muscle-bound, if not a little fatter, still wearing shorts no matter what the weather, and still bloody whistling.

When I think of Wack I recall an incident one afternoon in the Brooklands Club, when I was playing snooker with Chalkey. I happened to have a small hole in the back of my jeans, just underneath the pocket. Whilst I was bending over readying myself to pot a black ball and take my all-time highest score at snooker to eight, Wack came behind me, and slipped his fingers into the hole. With one quick pull, he ripped the entire leg of my jeans straight off. Without batting an eye, he calmly sat down at a table adjacent to where I was standing and took a sip of his pint; he never even glanced up at me. Everyone in the room burst out laughing including Chalkey.

I didn't flinch or say a word. I skilfully and sedately potted the blue—yes I missed the black—and joined Wack at the table. No words were spoken, and no acknowledgement of each other took place. This knocked Chalkey's duck off, and after several silent seconds, he proceeded to take his shot, still dumbfounded at my lack of response. When he bent over to align his aim, I gracefully approached him from the rear, and expertly ripped the two back pockets off his trousers in one swift movement. Such was the force of my actions his remaining pants came off too, leaving him with just his belt and underpants on. A giant eruption of laughter echoed around the room, and Chalkey stood there looking perplexed and ruffled—wearing his mother's knickers.

Within minutes of the game recommencing, Chalkey and me were down to our underwear; shirts, socks, shoes all destroyed. Following the final shot, we shook hands, and made our way home without as much as saying goodbye to anyone. Then Chalkey decided in his infinite wisdom that we didn't in fact need our underwear, so we both dispensed of them. Walking up Addison Road, stark-bollock naked in the middle of the afternoon, was a first for the pair of us. As I veered onto Linden Grove, Chalkey bid me farewell as he decided that he might as well collect the *Advertiser* from Johnny Hunt's, the nearby newsagents on his way home to save him time. Thinking nothing of this I kissed him sweetly and minced off into Redwood Drive.

Since the smoking ban came into force, I still find it strange that pubs and clubs no longer smell of stale tobacco and fag smoke. Having worked in the pub industry for over twenty-five years I am mortified that at least forty pubs are closing their doors every week in this economic meltdown we are currently experiencing. Recent figures indicate that beer sales have slumped to their lowest levels since the 'Great Depression' of the 1930s. What with the price of energy, raw materials and the discounted prices of supermarket beer, it's no wonder that pubs and clubs are struggling in the UK drinks sector. The pub is a British Institution and should be preserved for posterity. Back in the '70s pubs were full of people every day, and were the hub of the community. Landlords could make a decent living and were pillars of society. It was unthinkable not to go out on a weekend and not visit a hostelry and get totally rat-arsed. Even Uncle Tony, who brewed his own ale, frequented pubs in the nearby villages; he was barred from all his locals.

After the darts or snooker was over, me and the lads would settle down to a few *sherbets* and shoot the breeze, which usually meant discussing the forthcoming night's prospective shagging. Men and beer are a recipe for phenomenal bullshit on a grand scale. One evening in the Brooklands, a lovely looking lady entered, collecting money for some charity or another. Within minutes of arriving, she was quickly and expertly interfered with, losing her money and something a little more personal and precious, but I'd better not mention that Russ! She left the club a lot faster than she entered it and calm was restored. Then the 'Cockle Man' ventured in with his seafood; cockles, muscles, whelks, crabs, and other delicacies, like NSU and genital warts. I can still picture the guy in his white tunic carrying his wicker basket of goodies on his shoulders, dripping with sweat, no matter what the weather was outside. On this particular evening, Chalkey nicked some crab claws and stuffed them down his underpants. Then he asked one of the barmaids if she had any sugar for his pubic lice.

"Will it get rid of them?" she said gazing at the crab claws which were now in full view at the bar, protruding from his pants.

"No, but it'll rot their teeth and stop them biting my bollocks," was his reply.

Ten minutes had passed and the seafood seller stormed back into the club tap room and demanded that the thief who had stolen his crabs own up and return them. Just as he entered the room, Chalkey asked to see an amalgam filling that I'd had inserted into my back tooth earlier that day by the dentist. I thought nothing of his request and duly opened my mouth, only for him to shove one of the stolen claws in. Before I could spit it out, and remembering where it had just been, I was confronted by the cockle man. Chalkey ignored his appeals to turn out his pockets. During the exchange, the secretary of the club appeared and asked what all the commotion was about. The cockle man explained his dilemma, and said that he was short of a crab or two. At this I burst out laughing and out popped one of the man's missing nippers. I was asked to leave, and summoned to appear before the full committee the following week.

Committees in clubs were usually made up of cantankerous, mardy, whinging, thieving bastards who couldn't get a proper job. I'm sorry if I offend any existing or indeed residing committee members, but I can only speak of my personal experience. To cut a long story short I was barred from the club, simple as that. I didn't appeal as there seemed no point, but I did shit through the letter box of the chairman that same evening.

I remember once attending a club during a major alteration. This was prior to the rigorous standards of health and safety on site we now have to adhere to. My business partner Phil was with me and asked if he could use the toilets. The club secretary said that the toilets had been replaced, but if he went outside in the yard he could use the old ones. As my partner began to leave the room, the secretary told him that the door with a picture of a cock on was for the men. Phil looked somewhat shocked at this and said,

"Well if the men's toilet has got a cock drawn on for identification, what has the ladies' door got on it?"

"A picture of the Committee," was his reply.

Normally, around eightish, me and the lads used to nip over the road to the Toll Bar public house. This was a tenancy, run by a middle-aged couple. We always went into the public bar or 'Vaults', as it was referred to by my Grandad. Back then the price of beer was a few pence cheaper in the bar as opposed to the lounge, mainly due to the fact that the bar was a shit-hole. I always enjoyed drinking in the bar, because that's where all the characters hung out. Being a teenager in a pub full of real men was an excellent grounding for me. But you had to know your place, and not speak out of turn for fear of a thick ear.

I remember some great characters from this pub; Freddie, Dubba, Pip, Ringo, Daz, and Eddie; all equally bonkers but smashing chaps. Chalkey got barred one evening for showing his arse to the barmaid. *Mooning* was big in the '70s and at every opportunity Chalkey's rear was out on show for the world to enjoy. The landlady took exceptional offence to this and barred him for life. Chalks would stand outside in the rain looking through the window with big sad eyes, begging and pleading for forgiveness. Eventually, after massive pressure from all the lads, the landlady relented and let him back in; he'd been barred for about six months. Within twenty seconds of entering the public bar, he jumped onto a Britannia table and dropped his kecks. Needless to say, he never went in again.

When the time approached ten o'clock, we all downed our pints and made for the bus stop. Usually we'd be in the White Swan by quart past and that's when the real drinking started. Back then some of the boys would neck a gallon and a half of beer with relative ease. I was somewhat of a lightweight when it came to volume; my mind was on something different; women. I'd normally lost all my inhibitions by late evening and went into *skirt alert* mode; such was my obsession with the female form. I made sure I'd had enough beer to give me Dutch courage, but not too much to give me the *Brewer's Droop*. I wanted my tackle in working order; it had a good three-minute shift to do later that night. I know what you're all thinking, how did he manage to make it last a full three minutes? The answer is practice.

I'm not going to divulge any conquests that I may have had or mention any names as that would be showing off or blatant lying. The one thing that I can tell you is that I never went home alone to the *five-fingered widow*. Thinking back to the Toll Bar, I remember the one and only time I ever did a *runner* from a taxi without paying. Me and a bunch of guys had been on the piss in Sheffield, and had asked the driver to pull up outside the pub in the early hours of Saturday morning. We were a little the worse for wear, but full of mischief. Concocting a plan earlier that evening, we decided just to leg it when the taxi had come to a standstill. All went to plan, and as the taxi driver turned to me in the passenger seat to ask for the fare, I was off along with the rest of my mates from the back of the cab. Everything went as sweet as a nut, apart from my cousin Chivers running straight into the dwarf perimeter wall that surrounded the pub. His shins connected with the solid structure and he fell arse over tit, collapsing into the car park.

The taxi driver must have thought all his Christmases had come at once. He coolly and steadily made his way out of the driver's seat and into the car park, where he leathered Chivers from one end of it to the other. The fare should have been a tenner, but the taxi driver decided to rob him of all his cash, due to our disgraceful behaviour. If the driver would have been bothered to walk twenty yards further on he would have caught me as well. On watching poor old Chivers getting thrashed senseless, I couldn't move for laughing; I literally collapsed in a heap on the ground. It was marvellous watching him being volleyed around the pub grounds like a football. I couldn't quite make out what the taxi driver was saying to Chivers, but it did sound like he was calling him a thieving James Blunt.

Chapter 19
Nightclub Fervour

In 1977 a film called 'Saturday Night Fever' was released, starring John Travolta as Tony Manero. Tony is the king of his local discotheque, and his dancing helps him escape his mundane Brooklyn life. The film was a phenomenal global success and helped popularise disco music. Travolta became a household name, and all the guys wanted to emulate his style and dancing techniques. The soundtrack to the movie featuring songs by the Bee Gees became an all time best seller, and helped cement this flick as a classic of its genre.

Discos started popping up in every town, with young and old clambering to get in to strut their stuff. The dress code at the time was a three-piece matching suit for men—which I still have, and wear when I'm doing the vacuuming alone in the mornings. I was, and still am a useless dancer, blessed with Douglas Bader's feet, following his accident. I have no rhythm whatsoever, and the only dance I can slightly get away with is the *Wedding Dance*; the one where your legs are nailed to the floorboards and you shuffle a lot to give the impression that you've shit yourself. I've tried the *Twist* but jarred my knees and couldn't get up. I recently tried to participate in the *Woolly Bully* at our local manorial barn dance. When I came to kick out my foot, the brogue I was wearing came off like a tracer-bullet and hit a pensioner in her groin. I was mortified. It took me two hours to retrieve the shoe from her gusset after the paramedics had resuscitated her and the police had decided not to press charges of common assault against me. I now stick to tapping my feet quietly on the floor and humming.

The first nightclub I ever ventured into was called 'Scamps,' in Sheffield. Along with my mate Smig I was dressed as a cowboy, complete with toy guns, holsters, hats and high-heel boots. We must have looked like a right pair of dickheads, but we thought of it as the epitome of cool, and the height of vogue. The say fashion fades but style lasts forever. Going on what we were attired in that evening, our fashion faded before we'd even got out of the front door. The look wasn't so ridiculous, because within two minutes of walking through the front doors of the venue I'd pulled a nurse. My chat up line at the time was,

"Hey, you're my kinda woman....dirty!"

On reflection I know this sounded corny, demeaning and trite, but it worked. She was in my arms before you could whistle *Dixie* and within thirty minutes I was in the nurses' residence where she lived, giving her my version of *Rawhide*. I decided to try the 'Rodeo method'. This is where you take her from behind, and half way through the back-scuttle, tell her she's not as good a fuck as her sister. Then see how long you can stay on for.

Near to where I reside now used to be a small disco bar called the 'Charade,' at the Stag roundabout. It's where all the jailbait and underaged went. I remember bumping into Gary Glitter there

on numerous occasions in the '70s, before he started stalking playgrounds looking for his next wife.
Well he said his name was Gary Glitter, but on
reflection, he may have been lying, as he had ginger
hair and one leg. The Charade was the place to be
if you wanted to be seen. There was a pub opposite
called the Stag, and it was here that we ventured
before to going in the nightclub; well the drinks
were a lot cheaper and not watered down as much.
After spending an hour or so in the pub, several
parts pissed, we would stagger over to the Charade
following the scent of the vixens, which were all
on heat and gagging for it. Young boys and men
come to think of it, are pathetic in drink. Incredibly
our cocks grow twice as big; we last three times
as long in bed, and the women we've shagged over
the past months is times by a multiple of ten. In
reality we all have little or average dicks, last three
minutes—if we are lucky—and the women we have
shagged feature in our imagination and endless
masturbation.

Roxy Music and Bony M were the popular bands at the time, and I once won a dancing
competition in the Charade by mistake for a ren-
dition of a demented Cossack with chronic piles
dancing to the song *Rasputin*—how that wasp got
into my underwear is anyone's guess. Chalkey also
used to do a magnificent routine to *Let's Stick Together*
by Bryan Ferry and Roxy Music; it involved him
sticking his two front teeth out to mimic Ken Dodd,
and waving his arms about in a circular motion,
imitating a helicopter crashing. We all thought he
looked great, but we were daft. Without meaning to

sound a pretentious twat, I recently met Bryan Ferry in Faro Airport in Portugal. He still looks the bollocks and was a complete gentleman. He was being escorted by a personal stewardess onto the plane, but he still stopped to talk to me, which I thought was truly wonderful. I mentioned Chalkey's dance and the Charade, and he surprisingly asked me,

"Isn't that where Gary Glitter used to go?"

There used to be a top nightclub in Rotherham called 'Tiffanys'. I only frequented it twice before I was barred for life. Now let me explain. I actually had done nothing wrong. It was the people I happened to be with that night who caused all the trouble. My character was sullied and smeared that evening by the bouncers and management and I should have sued the bastards. Surrounding the dance floor were pseudo palm trees, complete with plastic coconuts to give the club an appearance of a Caribbean island. It looked more like a traffic island and nobody was really that impressed with the interior decoration. It was, however, large and full of *totty*, so it was the place to be seen.

On the way into the club, Smig and I bumped into a couple of local guys from Maltby who were a little older than us, called Tabs, Lunas and Coley. They were legends and all wild. No sooner had we got into the venue, Coley pretended to lose a glass eye, and had thirty or so people looking for it on the dance floor. What was really funny to us lot was every so often he would turn to face us, and close his other eye; he kept up the pretence of alternating eyes until one of the door men became wise to his trickery and threw him out. During his exit, he deliberately dropped some marbles onto the floor, and all hell broke loose with people shouting that they had found it.

After Coley had departed I was stood on the perimeter of the dance floor eyeing up potential skirt, when I heard a voice that sounded like it was coming from above. When I looked skywards, I was astonished to see Tabs and Lunas perched precariously up the palm trees. I think the melee that followed could have been averted if Tabs hadn't started throwing the plastic coconuts at the clubbers, and Lunas hadn't dropped his trousers and had a shit from a height of twelve feet. I was somewhat mesmerised by what I was witnessing. I was suspended in time, a mere onlooker in a surreal situation. Bouncers appeared from everywhere and war erupted between fellow clubbers and security men. Meanwhile, Lunas and Tabs were still out of reach in the tree tops, refusing to come down.

I know I have a tendency to look guilty, and I did start laughing hysterically, but there was no reason for a beefy bouncer to punch me straight on the chin and accuse me of causing the trouble. My dreaded curse had struck again. It had nothing at all to do with me; I was a mere bystander. What justification did he have for whacking me in the mouth? I protested my innocence, but it was to no avail. Several more doormen pounced on me and started putting the boot in. It was at this stage of the fracas that Lunas descended from the tree and landed on top of two of them. Lunas was a big bloke, and he flattened them; that evened the odds up nicely.

A lady then happened to scurry past me, carrying her 'Chicken in a Basket'. I swiped her hot chicken thigh, and rammed it into the guy's eye who had punched me. He yelped, more from the heat of the poultry I think, as opposed to the prod in his eye. It worked and he let me go. Now it was my turn. I did what all fair and honest fighters do in situations like these; I kicked him as hard as I could straight in the knackers, and he went down like a sack of spuds. I left him reeling around the dance floor like a dying fly.

I used to knock around with another guy who also went by the name of Smig—or Malc Smith as his real name was—who had been in the Royal Navy. Sadly he is no longer with us but he was a smashing lad. Good looking, funny, likable and a great mate. His brothers were also top blokes who went to the same primary school as Craig and I and were also in the scouts with us. Whilst on leave from the Navy, Malc had invited one of his fellow rear admirals to stay over with him in Maltby. The guy's name slips my memory, but he was the spitting image of the late and great actor Peter Lorre, complete with diminutive stature and boggly eyes.

I loved Peter Lorre specifically for his superb performance in 'The Hands of Orlac' where he plays a mad doctor, who performs a hand transplant for a pianist, but the hands were from a killer and have a mind of their own. Malc's mate's hands also had a mind of their own. One Friday evening we drove into Doncaster and made our way to the 'Seventh Heaven' night club. After aimlessly wandering around checking out what was on offer as far as the girls went, I caught site of the Lorre look-a-like, cavorting and gambolling on the dance floor with a group of older women. Back then it was common for women to put their hand bags in the middle of the dance floor and dance around them. I also remember people throwing salt onto the floor to aid n*orthern soul* dancing, but I never really understood the idea behind it; salt was something you put on your chips not on the bloody floor.

Lorre then took his shirt out of his trousers and began to squat over one of the larger hand bags, pretending to squirm and dance simultaneously. I hadn't a fucking clue what he was doing, but all the women were laughing and egging him on for more of the same. It wasn't like any kind of dancing I'd ever seen, and to be honest it looked for all intents and purposes that he was having a crap. His face began to contort and took on a sallow appearance. At one stage I actually thought that he was going to be sick. A voluptuous lady approached him and started to stroke his hair. He didn't flinch, and simply ignored her.

I was completely perplexed at his actions and couldn't fathom what the hell he was up to. After what seemed like an eternity, he slowly stood up and calmly walked off in the direction of the bar. Just as I was turning away from the dance floor, the sumptuous lady screamed out so loud it drowned the noise of the disco music. Startled, I spun round to see her looking directly into her hand bag. By now she had totally lost the plot and was shriek-ing and hollering, her face blood-red with the veins in her forehead about to burst. All the while she was pointing to the contents inside her bag. But I couldn't make out what she was saying, due to the colossal din she was making, and with the vicious tantrum she was throwing.

Bouncers and spectators alike appeared from nowhere and then the balloon went up. Basically, I was spot on the money with my first notion of what he was up to. On observing his strange behaviour over the bag, I suddenly realised that he had in fact crapped in her bag; my initial assumption unbelievably was proved to be correct. The moron had shit into the lady's receptacle. Now don't ask me why, as I've no chuffing idea. Why anyone would do such a thing was way beyond my thought process. I had just entered a new world, where the lunatics had taken over the asylum.

Pandemonium and chaos ensued and once again I was accused of being involved. I was as innocent as the poor lady, but for some strange reason the bouncers didn't concur with that. Four of the burly brutes picked me up by all my limbs and marched me straight towards the exit door. Instead of stopping to open the door, they opted for using my head as a battering ram. It was quite effective and certainly did the job. Just as they were about to toss me down a steep flight of stairs into the cold night air, I managed to say,

"Gentlemen, I take it that I'm leaving?"

I hit the ground like a sack of flour and in doing so sprained my wrist and chipped a tooth. My recalcitrant attitude to life changed that night. There was no point in arguing or causing even more trouble. The tawdriness of Lorre's actions was too much even for me to comprehend. He had gone beyond funny and ventured into the realms of stupidity and absurdity. After several minutes, I did think twice about giving one of the bouncers a kicking, but when I tried to stand up I soon realised that I'd broken my ankle.

Chapter 20
The European Experience

Hitch-hiking was very popular in my youth for getting around the country. I was fortunate enough to meet one of the greatest 'hitchers' of my generation, namely Spud Murphy. Spud was a legend in and around Maltby, a real cool, laid-back dude who was admired by almost everyone. Local folklore has it that Spud once hitched a lift from the White Swan Pub to Istanbul, without so much as stopping for a pee. He taught me that the key to successful hitching was to look the car or lorry driver straight in the face and smile, whilst moving your thumb slowly backwards in a tight circle. I practised this at home in my bedroom for months, perfecting the simultaneous smile and arm movement. My companion in globe-trotting was a close mate called Amos, who spent the same amount of time in his bedroom, pretending to draw a gun against himself in the mirror; he told me that he never once beat his reflection in the duels.

One evening in the Toll Bar we decided to try our luck at hiking around Europe. Having time on our hands, due to Amos being out of work and me awaiting a place at Art College, it seemed a perfect opportunity in quelling our respective travel-bug; we desperately wanted to follow Spud's footsteps and venture beyond the UK. Two of the regulars in the pub extended the hand of friendship, and generously offered us a lift down to Dover to assist us on our journey. It was rumoured that the guys in the tap room had taken it upon themselves to have a whip-round so that they could raise a few quid to get rid of us for a month or two, such was our popularity; subsequently they funded the petrol money for the outward excursion—a one-way trip so to speak. Looking back on this, I now realise what a favour I was undertaking by removing 'Amos the Undesirable' from Maltby, even if only for a short while.

The following morning, bags packed, we were ready to rock and roll. Our mutual friends picked us up at the bottom of Addison Road at 5.30am, and off we tootled, heading onto the M18, bound for Dover, only in all the excitement and fervour, we turned right instead of left and headed for Hull. After this minor blip and the ensuing argument of who was in charge of giving instructions, we came off at the first junction, and pointed the car in the correct direction. The journey zoomed by and at midday our buddies had dropped us off at the side of a dual carriageway and waved goodbye with two fingers. We were now left to our trusty smile and accompanying hand gestures.

Having eventually arrived in Dover, the initial thing we did was to grab lunch, which consisted of fish and chips. Sated and filled, Amos decided that a few jars in the nearby pub would help the planning process, so if was off to the Pilchard's Periwinkle for a session. The pub was old and dirty, and stank of stale fags and sailors' underwear; it was perfect, and we immediately felt at home, so much so, we stayed all day, and well into the night. Crashing on the beach at midnight we sought refuge underneath an upturned boat. Slipping into our respective sleeping bags, and utilising rucksacks for pillows, the boat provided shelter and privacy. Amos and I intended getting up at six in order to catch the first ferry to Calais.

Things didn't really go to plan. At midday, sun beating down and a packed beach of tourists surrounding us, we were somewhat alarmed at the predicament we found ourselves in. During the course of the morning the boat owner had retrieved his vessel and sailed away. What amazed and astounded me the most was the careful consideration the boat keeper had shown us by leaving us asleep, and not disturbing us. What a spectacle we must have looked; our anonymity stripped bare, cocooned in fleecy beds, dead to the world, while hundreds of holiday makers had pitched up around us. They were all in their bathing costumes and trunks, basking in the warm sunlight, happily building sand castles and munching on ice cream, and we were trussed up, sweating our tits off in the middle of them all, clothes on, asleep like two vagrants.

I nudged Amos and alerted him to our situation. Trying desperately not to draw any further attention or embarrassment, we calmly folded our bedding up and stowed it in the rucksacks. This was followed by a quick stretch and testicle assembly, and we gingerly made our way off the beach in search of the ferry terminal, whistling nonchalantly and looking skywards.

Two hours on from our beach debacle we were in France. What struck me most about France was the language; it was French, and I didn't understand a word of it. French cannot be a difficult language to grasp though, as I heard loads of small children speaking it. Hitch-hiking from Calais to Paris proved rather more difficult than we first expected; everything Spud had taught me seemed to be wasted on the French drivers. Even the English tourists blatantly ignored our pleas for lifts.

Having 'thumbed' for four hour and got nowhere, we started to walk to Paris, as it seemed a more sensible option. After fifteen or so miles it started to get dark so we decided to set up camp at the side of the road. It was at this point of the trip that I should have realised what a complete cluster-fuck the journeying around Europe was going to be. Amos, in his infinite wisdom, had left the tent on the beach in Dover. He said he simply forgot it. We drank the last of our cheap wine and slumped on the grass verge adjacent the roadside, completely fagged out from our efforts.

Early next morning we were awoken by the sound of a road sweeper, considerately and accurately flicking up all the detritus from the highway over our faces. It had the desired effect, and we quickly adopted our hiking routine again. Then the first lorry to pass us suddenly hit the brakes and came to a standstill some twenty yards away, smoke billowing from the back of his tyres. Amos and I stood there aghast and bewildered. The guy beckoned us up into his cab and off we went on our merry way to Paris. After half a mile he asked Amos in his thick Bretagne accent if he fancied a blow job; normally Amos would have succumbed to the man's charms, but he was French and dirty looking. The lorry juddered to a halt, and we clambered out as fast as we could. Our first experience left us shell-shocked.

Two hours later we were back in transit, only this time with a normal guy. He drove us all the way to the outskirts of the capital city, and bid us au revoir by kissing us both full on the mouth for several (more than a few but slightly less than a bunch) minutes. We casually strolled into the centre all smug-like after this unusual show of affection. I didn't realise the French were so kind and compassionate.

The sunbeams were dancing on the lazy river and the temptation to take a quick wash in the Seine proved too much for the pair of us. Having bathed in sewage, we sought food and wine from a nearby store. As we munched the last of the dry French stick and swilled back the cheap plonk like proper epicureans, our attention switched to a young lad who looked extremely stressed and agitated. He made his way over to where we were sitting, and explained that having just arrived in the city, some thieving bastard had stolen his wallet with all his money in. I genuinely felt sorry for the guy, but Amos took an instant dislike to him because he had ginger hair.

Having ignored his appeals for money and wine, we left him crying in the gutter; he'd tried quaffing Amos' red wine without asking. Big mistake. Amos leathered him there on the spot. Nobody came between Amos and his *vino-collapso*. Apparently he was never seen again; it was rumoured that Amos buried him alongside the 'Unknown Soldier' underneath the Arc de Triomphe. Later that evening we sought refuge in a park, adjacent the river. When we arrived, to our surprise, we came across a group of hikers laid out on the ground in the shape of a star, with their heads all touching. They explained to us that the park was a regular haunt of *cottagers* and *turd-burglars* so we took their advice and joined the circle.

Next morning we did the touristy bit and visited all the major Parisian landmarks, witnessing some breath-taking architecture in the process. To me, Paris is definitely the most beautiful city in Europe, after Sheffield. We met up with a guy called 'Black Vince' who spoke fluent French but was a total piss-artist. Vince was last seen trying to hack off a piece of metal from the Eiffel Tower with my pen knife, for me to take home as a souvenir. After another night in 'Penis Park' we made our way out of the city and headed for Belgium. A record producer from Marseilles stopped for a pee break and asked us to join him, on the proviso that Amos drove his car, as he was shattered. To add to this, he informed us that he was late for an appointment in Amsterdam and would we like to come along? Amos and me took one look at each other and nodded simultaneously; Amsterdam here we come.

Paris was beautiful. Belgium was flat. Having bypassed the country purported to resemble a 'Witch's tit', our sleepy passenger/driver dropped us off on the outskirts of Utrecht; due to an impromptu business meeting there he'd neglected to mention to us. We still needed to travel quite a distance to reach our intended destination of Amsterdam.

No sooner had we raised a thumb, a Volkswagen camper van complete with two Aussie head cases stopped to give us a ride. These dudes were the *mutt's nuts;* great guys who lived for the moment. Within minutes we were best of buddies, and our new friendship lasted nearly a week. They supplied us with food, drink, a canvas shelter and chicks; yes chicks. They picked up a *Sheila* or three for us to play with on route such was their charm, charisma and good looks. The camper van was alive with activity of all sorts, and we thought we'd reached heaven. The *Sheilas* turned out to be Israelis, part way through an all expenses trip paid for by the government, prior to them undertaking their national service training. They were hot to trot, and who were we to stop them taking advantage of a couple of naive Yorkshire lads, desperate for sex.

The next few days saw Amos and me exhausted from the insatiable appetite of the Israeli nymphets. We didn't leave the camp site, not even for nourishment, as we were getting all the sustenance we needed right there. I was sad to see the girls depart, but it allowed us time to recuperate. The following day we sauntered into the city and sought sanctuary in the notorious red light district. If you ever get a chance to visit this part of Amsterdam please do so; some of the sights are incredible. The women come in all shapes and sizes, and the transsexuals are indistinguishable, as Amos will testify. He pulled what he thought was a girl in one of the numerous windows that open onto the canal side, and was duly escorted inside. Five minutes later he came out looking all flush, with beads of sweat glistening on his forehead.

"What's the matter mate?" I asked all concerned.

"I'd rather not go there," he snapped back.

I pushed him a little harder for more inside carnal knowledge of his sexual exploit.

"Come on pal, you can share your secrets with me. No one will ever know," I reassured him.

"Well if you promise not to breathe a word I'll tell you. No sooner had I released the best pair of top bollocks I'd ever seen, she was down there giving me oral sex, which was amazing. She could have sucked the Thames dry; it was like a vacuum," he whispered to me.

"Go on then, what else happened? Why do you look so sheepish and pale?" I pressed on.

"Well, it was all going to plan until she/he slipped his gigantic cock out and asked me to reciprocate," he said, pulling a face that was about to throw up.

"You mean to tell me that you've just had a *goolie-gobble* with a *he/she*? Jesus wept mate; wait until the lads hear about this back home, it'll blow their minds," I said.

"If it's any consolation, it's just frigging blown mine. I feel as if I've been artificially incinerated," Amos retorted.

I promised not to mention a word; that was until now. Amos once said that I couldn't hold my piss, and to prove him right I have now shared his dirty, despicable secret with the world. For this I am truly sorry, but sometimes a man's got to do what a man's got to do, and I'm great at dishing out other people's vile indiscretions. Knowing Amos like I do, I'm sure he'll see the funny side of it; after all, he's now divorced from Derek, and will thrive on the sordid publicity this story will bring to his tap room cronies.

Amsterdam was wonderful in every sense of the word. Bleary-eyed and massively hung over from a week of sex, drugs and rock and roll, we left our Aussie mates and headed for the German border. Entering Germany back in the early '80s was an ordeal in itself; it would have been easier getting over the Berlin Wall. We were extremely fortunate in hitching a ride with a theologian family who resided in Duisburg. They felt sorry for us and under-standing the plight we were in trying to enter their homeland, kindly offered us a lift. Getting through border control was a lot easier with a German family, especially one who spoke fluent English as well. Safely through, they further extended the hand of friendship by taking Amos and I to their house for dinner.

The 'Family Baker' as they were known, turned out to be fabulous and generous hosts. They treat-ed us like royalty and made me and Amos feel at home immediately. Being strong religious types, they fed and watered us whilst constantly checking we were okay. Nothing was too much trouble for them; it was as if they were trying to make amends for something that they had done to offend or upset the pair of us. Their hospitality held no bounds and we ended up staying with them for several days.

When we said our goodbyes they gave me a tent, a packed lunch and a fistful of German marks. I was speechless; their only request to us was that if their grandchildren ever visited the UK in years to come, we had to promise to show them the same cordial friendship. As I left their driveway tears filled my eyes; no one had ever shown me such unconditional warmth, love and care.

We made our way to the train station and Amos asked how much money Frau Baker had stuffed into my hands. I told him it was the equivalent of twenty quid. He looked at me earnestly and said,

"Tight *kraut* bastards. Twenty-fucking-quid between the pair of us; is that all?"

Amos could sometimes get on my tits big style, and his flippant, ungrateful comment ratcheted up my anger to boiling point. It's the nearest I ever came to smashing his teeth down his throat. I reminded him of the fact that we had only brought thirty pounds with us for our entire trip, which we estimated would be for a period of approximately six weeks. I did this whilst standing on his neck with my size nines pressing firmly down on his jugular. He quickly saw the errors of his ways and apologised. Still filled with rage, I just let his apology pass; it was way beyond my comprehension that somebody could be so selfish and unappreciative. I then realised Amos had passed out.

Leaving Germany was a wrench for me personally, and I'll never forget the charitable nature of the family who looked after us. We took a short train journey back over the border into Holland, and after two days hiked our way into Belgium, arriving very late one summer evening. I recall the night as being jet-black with total cloud cover. We clumsily clambered over a high wire fence and pitched our tent on a flat piece of grass which had a vague similarity to that of a garden lawn. Knackered from the walking, we hit the hay and were sound asleep in seconds.

The following morning I was awoken by the sound of people milling around outside the tent. I nervously peered out to see what all the commotion was about. To my total amazement, I was surprised to find a bunch of smartly dressed office workers, looking equally astonished at our presence. It suddenly dawned on me—well it was early morning—that we had inadvertently made camp in front of a large office complex on an industrial estate. Our tent was pitched on the land surrounding the building, which was indeed a well manicured lawn. What a spectacle we must have appeared to them; they arrive for work to be met by a pair of vagrants camped out on their beautifully landscaped gardens. Fortunately they did see the funny side of our predicament, and invited us in for lemon tea and croissants.

Belgium is a country full of promise, yet delivers very little other than great chocolate and beer. I'd never been in a bar elsewhere with such an extensive menu for the beer on offer. One particular bar in Bruges had three hundred different beers on sale from around the world. I recently visited Bruges again after many years and it's still a beautiful city, offering a proliferation of quality bars and exquisite chocolate shops; bugger all else mind you. Our time in Belgium was pretty uneventful, and we hopped over back into France.

After spending several weeks under canvas with Amos, his little idiosyncrasies began to get on my nerves; especially his nail clicking habit and whistling songs out of tune. France first time around was exciting and stimulating. Phase two just didn't hit the spot for me, so I decided that I was going to make my way home. Amos seemed genuinely put out, but agreed that it was time to make tracks back to *Blighty*.

Sun-tanned and dishevelled we arrived in Dunkerque in the middle of what resembled a skin-head rally full of neo-Nazis. I must admit, walking through the gauntlet of muscle-bound, leather-clad, handlebar moustached macho guys made my arse twitch for one reason or another. Amos was stopped by a guy who said his name was Dick Blower; his companion was known as Richard Beater. We both laughed nervously and minced off at breakneck speed. When we finally entered the ferry terminal, Amos told me that he was overcome with a rush of mixed emotions at meeting these gentlemen; I've never felt the same again about Amos.

As we boarded the ferry, I noticed a crowd of people surrounding a woman lying on the floor. I could vaguely make out some of them saying how ridiculous and embarrassing it was seeing someone so drunk and out of control. Being a nosey bastard, I pushed my through to the front of the crowd and immediately realised that the woman in question wasn't drunk at all, but that she was in the throes of an epileptic fit.

Typical English snobbery and ignorance was stopping fellow passengers aiding this unfortunate lady, so I quickly stepped in and comforted her best I could. To my great relief she stopped convulsing and began to come round. It was then that I noticed the blood on the side of her cheek and eye. It was obvious to me that in during the seizure she must have fallen face first onto the marble floor. Eventually two paramedics arrived on the scene and before you could say "Dick Blower" I was whisked off in an ambulance to the nearby hospital cradling my damsel in distress. I remember Amos saying that he would look after my gear and wait for me in the lounge area of the terminal.

Speeding through the streets of France on the way to the hospital, I suddenly realised that I had no means of identification, no money, was in the company of someone I'd never met and no means of getting back to the port. The paramedics ignored my pleas and stayed focused on the injured lady, who by now was squeezing the life out of my hand. She was stretchered off to theatre, and I was left in the waiting area. Several hours passed. I did think about doing a runner, but where to and which way? My French was minimal and with no means of transport, I decided to stay put, which seemed the lesser of two evils. Just after 11.00pm, my new girl friend appeared from behind a screen, bandaged up like a *mummy*.

"Hey, what's yer face, come over here. I need you to get me back to the ferry terminal now! We've got to be on the midnight crossing, or else the shit will hit the proverbial," she whispered to me.

Stunned by her words and appearance, I snaffled a green gown off the back of a chair adjacent reception, draped it over her shoulders, and made for the exit. By a stroke of luck, a cabbie had just dropped off his passengers and was totting his francs up. I bundled my wounded pup into the back of the taxi and uttered some guttural shite which sounded a little French accompanied by some wild hand gestures trying to describe sailing. It seemed to do the trick, and before long we were back in the terminal building.

Amos was exactly where I'd left him, only this time he was totally shit-faced, having necked a gallon of wine; he'd located my wallet from inside my rucksack and emptied it of the contents. Amos was good like that. By the skin of our teeth, all three of us boarded the ferry, and off we set, homeward bound. My acquaintance then explained to the pair of us that she was a spy. *Billy Bullshitter* sprang to mind, but when she elaborated on her story, it did sound pretty convincing and genuine. She treated us to a late snack and oodles more drink before departing to her cabin. She thanked me personally for acting in the way I did, and pressed a bunch of pound notes into my hand. I kissed her on both her cheeks—well I was still in the French mindset— and told her to think nothing of it.

I never saw the lady again, even though I waited until all the passengers had disembarked the following morning. I counted up the dosh she'd given me and it added up to the princely sum of forty quid, which was more than we'd brought with us six weeks earlier. Hitch-hiking back up the

M1 home, I couldn't help wondering what might have happened if me and the spy would have been apprehended in the hospital; me with no means of identification, and her, the 'secret squirrel'. Maybe the French police would have locked me up with the 'Dunkerque dick-skinners'. My bowels would have definitely left my body.

Chapter 21
Arty-Farty

Having arrived back in Maltby after my adventures in mainland Europe, I had a reality check and decided after all that I wanted to go to Art College; students seemed to have an easy life and that suited me down to the ground. I enrolled in the one-year foundation course at Rotherham College of Arts and Technology. The main objective of the course was to prepare you for higher education in art and design, culminating in an honours degree. Art was the only subject I excelled at during my school days.

The course offered a broad series of project-based art and design units. These different disciplines ranged from life drawing, ceramics, graphic design, to photography; I think that there were at least twelve alternative study modules, all of which I loved. For the first time in my life I was actually doing something I was both good at and enjoyed. No more mind-numbing mathematics or boring biology. The icing on the cake for me was during my first lesson, I was joined by another great pal known as Steve 'Fishy-fingers', or 'Fingers' for short; he'd also signed up.

Fingers and I met at Maltby Comprehensive, and I'm glad to say that we are still the best of mates. Student life turned out to be a lot more arduous than I initially expected. The amount of work we had to do was colossal, and the entire grant for the year was £36

I know I shouldn't moan, as students nowadays get bugger all, other than a massive debt to start their careers off with. My course cost nothing, and to me, higher education should still cost nothing. Investing in people, both young and old, but especially the young, makes perfect economical sense. Having to pay tuition fees sucks in my opinion, as does getting debt-ridden for the rest of your life. I personally know bright kids who have missed out on further education due to the financial obstacles placed in their paths when leaving school. Talented individuals should be properly supported because an educated manpower is our future.

The government has set a ludicrous objective by stating that half the population should go to university. Too many further education establishments purporting to be universities are offering students *Mickey-Mouse* degrees with no prospects of jobs at the end of the course. Students need to obtain degrees that will help them get real jobs in society at large; basically, the government is lying to them, making unsustainable promises. The only thing guaranteed when leaving higher education is massive debt. We should be preparing scholars for careers that matter, not assisting them in gaining '*ology-degrees* worth jack-shit.

It has been forecast that in 2010 the government will remove the cap on tuition fees, almost doubling them; this will be catastrophic for potential students wanting to go to university. Everyone should be given the opportunity to go on to higher education, but only if they are academically capable enough, when the fees are realistic and the course is geared to generate real jobs. Lying to a generation about the advantages of going to university needs to stop right now, before it's too late.

Obviously someone has to pay to keep universities running and in business, because that it what it is, a business. In America, some of the academic institutions have a 'blind means test' where the best scholars pay what they can afford; the rest will invariably come from the tax payer. We live in a world where there is such a premium placed on knowledge, and we here in Britain have to play a major role in leading the global economy by investing and nurturing talent within our universities, because in reality, we will be investing in our economy. Everyone who can benefit from further education should benefit from it. Universities are places of academic excellence; a stepping stone to a better career.

Now that I've blown up all the arses of the whinging, debt-ridden, moaning, idle, drugged-up, booze-addled, lazy student bastards out there, who spend all their parents hard earned cash on shite and not my book; if the student population of the UK don't invest in my little piece of literature, I will personally beat the crap out of every ginger haired student I ever meet from now on. You have been warned wasters.

Getting off my soap-box and back to Art College, the short time I spent at Rotherham was extremely satisfying and very intense. I would regularly work through the night building up my portfolio readying myself for polytechnic. Rotherham had a great reputation for preparing students and getting them into first time placements at 'polys'. Fingers and I played off each other all the time with our fellow students. One Monday morning I announced to our group that Fingers had passed away that previous weekend. We even had a whip-round for his funeral such was my ability to be creative with the truth. One particular girl burst into tears, declaring her undying love for him. The following morning, Fingers calmly strolled into the design studio larger than life; on seeing him, the girl in question fainted. Our warped sense of humour did piss most people off, but we didn't give a damn.

During an interval in a life drawing class, our model, who happened to have more scars on her body than a Vietnam War veteran, casually walked over to where Fingers was situated and leant over his easel to view his work. She was entirely naked and I noticed how uncomfortable Fingers was by her close proximity. To make matters worse, her nipples were stuck out like fighter pilots' thumbs, and touching the side of his face. Fingers turned to politely ask her to move away, and inadvertently brushed his lips over her erect nipples. She pretended to be startled, but absolutely loved it. Fingers, however, had to be excused from the room to be sick. She was in her seventies!

On another occasion, we both happened to be in the dark room during a photography lecture. Trying very hard to concentrate on the task at hand, which was difficult under the circumstances—one of my fellow students had her hand down my crotch choking my chicken—I accidently knocked a tray of photographic fixer all over the floor. Our tutor heard the commotion and on realising what had happened shouted,

"Don't worry, I'm coming."

"So is Alf, by the looks of it," Fingers laughingly remarked.

Every Friday after college, a group of students went to Herringthorpe Leisure Centre to play five-a-side football on the outdoor pitches there. On one particular evening, Fingers turned out for us, as we were a man short. Now I need to explain that Fingers is as blind as a bat without his *gigs* on, so seeing him standing there minus his spectacles was quite unnerving; how would he see the ball coming? Five minutes into the game, Fingers set off like a bat out of hell chasing what he thought was the ball; in reality it turned out to be a starling flying over the pitch.

All I can recall is seeing him running straight into the cross-bar of the goalposts at the speed of sound, rendering him instantly unconscious. The dull, loud thud of his skull connecting with the steel tubular bar made me cringe in pain. How and why he didn't see something six-inches in diameter running nine-feet across still beats the hell out of me, but as I said before, without his glasses he was virtually blind. It took me five minutes to bring him round; in fairness to the lad, that he carried on playing for the team that night was testament to his commitment to the cause. To help his situation, we made him goalkeeper so he wouldn't have to run around.

By the second half, he had actually bucked up a little, and stopped being sick. One of our opponents lofted a ball straight over Fingers into the back of the net. Fingers didn't even see the player, let alone the ball. When we explained to him that he'd let a goal in he was devastated. As he turned to retrieve the ball from the back of the net, instead of bending down and simply picking it up, he swung on the cross-bar with both hands and feebly tried to bring the ball back with his feet. It was as if we were seeing what happened next in slow motion, but there was nothing anyone could do to stop it. As Fingers lurched forwards in pursuit of the ball, the entire framework of the goal posts tilted in the opposite direction, crashing to the ground with Fingers' fingers trapped underneath. Once again a resonating thud shuddered around the ground. Poor old Fingers was in agony, pinned down by the bar across his hands. It took us several minutes to free him, due to me and the other team members being bent over double with laughter, unable to move a muscle.

Art College is a magic place to be, if you genuinely love painting and drawing like I do. Even though the course was full on I still managed to get my assignments done on time. One lesson that I wasn't too bothered about was still life classes, drawing fruit and the likes. Friday was 'Fruit Day', and during one lesson I got so bored I decided to paint over my entire canvas in ultramarine blue. I've always been a fan of blue whatever the shade is.

My tutor at the time didn't share my passion. She thought that I'd spoiled a relatively decent painting and was just pissing around, and told me so. I ignored her remarks and leant backwards to admire my work at a distance. In doing so, I toppled over several demountable screens, separating two different classes. The adjoining class was part way through an exam, so when the screen came crashing down on their unsuspecting craniums, all hell broke loose. The Chancellor of the college threatened to sue me, and wouldn't accept that it was an accident. Fingers didn't help matters by pretending to be injured in the incident; he suddenly developed a limp which lasted a fortnight. I had to carry his bags to college during his feigned recovery period. I did however, wreak my revenge at the end of the semester.

Having chosen as my main subject Three-Dimensional Design, specialising in Interior Design, and having been verbally accepted at Leeds Polytechnic, the pressure on me somewhat abated, whilst for Fingers, who hadn't been offered an opening yet, it intensified. I took full advantage of this by being a pain in the arse to him, in every sense of the word. School-boy humour has always been top of my list, playing practical jokes on people, especially close friends. The simple act of placing a drawing pin on someone's chair fills me with enormous glee.

During a graphic design lesson, I asked Fingers to get me a coffee from the canteen. He duly obliged, failing to notice on his return that I'd placed a drawing pin on his seat. He handed me my beverage and with a red-hot coffee in his hand dropped like a lead weight onto the pin. It was like watching a rocket going into orbit such was the speed of his ascent. Coupled with this he spilled his molten refreshment straight over his bollocks for good measure. It was priceless. I've never seen someone disrobe to their *kecks* so quickly in my life. His testicles swelled to the size of swedes, and were a perfect colour match, being purple. I howled with delight at his misfortune, and did the honourable thing by blaming someone else. He didn't have to pretend to limp anymore, as he was so bow-legged, he couldn't have stopped a pig in a *gennel (covered alleyway)*.

I left art college knowing that I wanted to pursue a career connected with art in some way or another, and readied myself for my forthcoming degree at Leeds. Fingers went on to be a porno-photographer based in Thurcroft. My neighbour David, who visits him every week for 'Cross-Dress Friday', shoots over there with our local parish priest.

Chapter 22
Ladybower Reservoir

During the summer holidays prior to starting polytechnic, me and a bunch of the boys decided that a male bonding weekend was necessary. Our choice of destination was the Peak District, an upland area in northwest England, mainly in northern Derbyshire. It forms the southern end of the Pennines, which according to my Grandad should have been bombed flat during the Second World War—to stop it raining over Maltby. It is an area of outstanding beauty and is a National Park covering approximately 550 square miles.

The main roads running through the Park are the A57 Snake Pass, and the A628 Woodhead Pass. When the weather's fine and the roads are relatively clear of traffic, these networks allow you to drive through vast areas of breathtaking scenery as stunning as anywhere in the world. The problem with both these passages is that they are almost permanently congested with big stupid lorries and caravans, making driving through the Peak District a pain in the arse; oh, and when we get a flutter of snow, both routes are immediately closed to traffic by the authorities.

We met up at the Miner's Institute at eleven o'clock on Saturday morning and got stuck into some serious drinking. My mate Unzi had hired a Bedford transit van with roller-shutter doors;

completely inappropriate for the seven journey-
men, but hellishly cheap according to him. Unzi
didn't need to drink to act daft, as he was as mad
as a frog to start with. At chucking out time, we
all scrambled into the back of the van, laden down
with more cans of booze. Our first port of call was
going to be Ladybower Reservoir, for some skinny-
dipping.

Ladybower Reservoir was the third and last of a
series of reservoirs which were built in the Upper
Derwent Valley. The dam wall holds back approximately 6310 million gallons of water, making it the
largest of the three. Two villages were sacrificed to
make way for Ladybower Reservoir; Derwent and
Ashopton. I recently visited Ladybower during a
drought and was delighted to have seen the tops
of some of the buildings of Derwent village at the
northern end of the reservoir poking up through
the water.

The reservoirs of the Derwent Valley are most
famous for the fact that they were used by the 617
squadron, the 'Dambusters', to practise their bomb-
ing raids in 1943, prior to their mission to the Ruhr
Dams in Germany. The movie 'The Dambusters'
was also filmed there. We knew an old guy called
Big Jim who witnessed these training sessions and
he thought the squadron was just pissing around
and joy-riding. Dr. Barnes Wallis designed the
'bouncing' bomb which was an incredible piece of
ingenuity and engineering. The RAF flew over the
dams practising the release of the makeshift bombs
at specified heights and speeds. Big Jim blamed
the RAF for knocking the chimney stack down

off his farm house and scaring his geese so much they stopped laying eggs altogether. He was furious with the *Brylcreem boys* and tried shooting at their planes with his 12-bore. He was arrested for being a subversive and a *quisling,* and imprisoned for ten years, which in my mind was a fair carriage of British justice. He used to walk in a goose-stepping fashion, which could have been misconstrued for being a Nazi supporter, and he did sport a little 'Hitler' style moustache; his defence with regards to the facial hair was that he'd grown the moustache first.

After travelling in the back of a van with five other drunks and unable to see of the outside world, I decided that we needed to stop to take a leak. Banging on the wall of the transit to attract Unzi's attention proved fruitless, so we took it on ourselves to carefully open the shutter door and pee out of the back whilst the van was in motion. This would have been fine if we had happened to be in the countryside and not the centre of Sheffield; we estimated that we'd been travelling miles, and this proved not to be the case. I still think that we may have got away with urinating out of the back door of a moving vehicle, if right behind us there hadn't been a police car. It beggars belief that two of us started pissing from a height straight onto the bonnet of the *jam-sandwich* with two bewildered coppers inside. The car's siren immediately came on, deafening us in the process.

Unzi had no idea why he was being pulled over outside the main railway station by the police and was as shocked as they were when he realised what we had just done. Fortunately for us the police were obviously busy on some other case that day, only cautioned all seven of us, asking us to appear at Maltby nick first thing Monday morning. Being half-cocked from the effects of the afternoon session we all pretended to be apologetic and promised to return home immediately, bowing our heads and looking sorrowful for our inappropriate actions. When the *fuzz* zoomed off out of sight, we thought "Fuck em," and carried on discharging projectile urine onto the streets of Sheffield, before heading on towards our intended destination of the Ladybower Inn for some more refreshment.

On reaching our hostelry we found it closed, which was a bit of a pisser. One of the lads named Spot decided that he needed to shit, and the reservoir looked a better option than most for emptying his bowels. He quickly disrobed and like a leaping salmon ran to the water's edge and dived straight in, not realising the severe cold temperature of the reservoir. Within thirty seconds he was back on dry land shivering and minus his pooh. He staggered up the bank side onto the main carriageway, stark naked and wet through. Unbelievably, the same policemen who had pulled us over in the city centre turned up outside the Ladybower Inn. They looked even more gobsmacked than we did. Getting out of their vehicle, one of the coppers looked straight at Spot and said,

"Have you been swimming?"

I know that policemen are not the sharpest tools in the box, but here was a lad, buck-naked, water dripping off him, standing adjacent a lake in the middle of the road. Spot took one look at him and simply replied,

"No."

I had to go behind the van to hide conceal my laughter; it was a priceless remark. The officer, accepting Spot's answer asked him to get dressed. Spot obliged by putting his brogues on; nothing else, just his shoes. The sight of Spot and the police stood there in the middle of the road discussing the whys and wherefores of the dangers of swimming in a reservoir, with Spot proclaiming his innocence was just excellent. The chance of being caught twice in the same day by the same bobbies was almost too much to take in. The icing on the cake was that they accepted his fabricated story of shitting himself in the van, and let him off with a further caution.

Spot was overjoyed at not getting arrested for being drunk and disorderly whilst nude in public. As he waved the police goodbye with his wanger, he inadvertently stood in the biggest pile of fresh dog shit imaginable; I feel justice was served. Talking of wangers, one of the other lads on the trip was a guy called Ben, who was the shy retiring type. He happened to be stood next to me behind the van whilst the pair of us relieved ourselves of even more urine. When I glanced down at him, my eyes nearly popped out. His willy was like a baby's arm with an apple stuck on the end. I think Bazza would have come second in a nob competition, such was Ben's *Hampton*. I couldn't help wondering, gazing at the enormity of it, whether or not he could suck his own cock. I didn't need to wait long for my answer as Spot saw exactly what I was looking at and asked him outright.

"Oye Ben, can you suck yer sen off mate?"

Ben raised his eyes to the pair of us and simply smiled; his face spoke volumes. Spot nudged me and whispered,

"The lucky bastard. I have to get my dog to do me."

Well that's enough about Ben's massive cock and Spot's bestial connections. We all piled back into the van and it was off to Castleton for the evening. But every time that we drove into a pub car park the landlord was waiting for us at the entrance to bar us. This happened on five occasions, and we began to think that we would never get another drink that night. That was until we stumbled on a little pub in Hathersage, run by a complete wino known as 'Red-Eye'.

He was a marvellous host who showered us with his cordial nature, and his phlegm. Once inside, he shut the curtains and locked the door; we knew we were in for a mammoth session of drinking.

"Help yourselves guys, the drinks are on me tonight. Everything is free, as much as you want," he said whilst showering us with even more spittle.

I remember Unzi saying that there was a God, and we all went around the bar servery and got stuck in. We subsequently found out later that night that Red-Eye was not only a drunk, he was also a bankrupt drunk; that same day the bank had foreclosed on him. He was about to notify the Brewery, but decided to get arse-holed instead. We just happened to be at the right place at the right time. *By gum* did we get shit-faced that night, and well into the next morning. Red-Eye collapsed in a heap on the floor of the taproom, and Ben very considerately emptied his pockets of all his change, whilst Unzi emptied the till of all its cash. The thing that strikes me still about Maltby boys is that we are all thieving, greedy bastards underneath when it comes to free ale. With regards to the theft of the cash, there's no excuse. Unzi and Ben were just robbing twats, but they did have the decency to share their spoils with the rest of us later that day when buying fish and chips, proving that they weren't all bad.

Chapter 23
My Mate Neville

Periodically I have been blessed with having special friends in my lifetime. One of those who particularly stood out for me was a guy I met at college, called Neville Rowley. Nev was a one-off. He once described himself to me as 'an albino Woody Allen', and that was a fair description of him. I was fortunate to be on the same Interior Design course as Neville, and subsequently lodged with him for two years on Stanmore Place in Leeds. Nev was so different to anyone I'd ever met before. He was eccentric, caring, intelligent and self-opinionated but I loved being with him. Sometimes he'd drive me up the wall, but the majority of the time he had me in stitches with his antics. He was a chap who never outwardly tried to be funny; it just came naturally to him.

During 'Fresher's Week' at Leeds in 1981, I happened to bump into a diminutive, thin guy spouting off about how good at snooker he was. On looking at this gaunt young man, and noticing his *jam-jar bottom* glasses, I decided to introduce myself. After telling me his name was Nev, he carried on addressing his audience, which comprised of a set of geeks and nerds. I was fascinated at how he held court, but didn't happen to be speaking to any of them directly; he had his back to the lot of them.

As he wittered on, I soon realised that the ensemble were definitely listening to his conversation, and occasionally taking part in it, but all the while, Nev wasn't facing them. I approached Nev from the side, and he didn't move a muscle. When I fronted him face to face he suddenly jumped back, and told me not to creep up on him like that again. I subsequently found out that Neville had both his eye lenses taken out as a child and suffered from tunnel vision. I didn't know whether or not he was joshing me, so I moved to the side of him.

"You've gone again mate. Come back into my field of vision," he said to me.

Still not really knowing his game plan, I suggested we had another drink at the bar. Now what I didn't know at our early meeting was that Nev couldn't hold his booze; two pints and he was anybody's, three and he was everybody's. Within fifteen minutes of swigging his pint down we found ourselves in an altercation with a group of bouncers. Nev had apparently told one of them he was an expert in Judo, and had offered to fight him. The guy laughed it off, but he proceeded to insult him by suggesting that we—Neville and I—would fight four security men who were manning the doors to the Students Union bar. Here we go again I thought to myself; I've known this bloke less than an hour and now I'm going into battle with him against several apes. Why did I attract trouble so easily?

Deciding to use my newfound brain, I thought the best course of action would be to negotiate our way out of the impending beating. I sat Neville down on a bar stool, and asked him to remain there.

I then explained to the bouncers that he'd had his drink spiked and didn't know what he was doing or saying. Miraculously they believed me and sauntered off. The relief I felt was orgasmic. I turned to where I'd left Nev to notify him of our imminent departure. Alas my new buddy had disappeared. He was nowhere to be seen. I didn't have to wait long to locate him. I heard a fracas near the toilets and hurried over to catch what was going down; Neville as it turned out.

Apparently, whilst I was arbitrating with the door men, he had picked an argument with the bartender. It later came to my knowledge that this guy had taken his false teeth out and stuck them on the end of Nev's nose with chewing gum. Yes, you're right; and I haven't got a bleeding clue, so don't even think of going there. Neville ended up getting punched on the jaw, and the barman, who was now surrounded by a group of his mates, started laughing at poor Nev's plight. This really pissed me off, so in for a penny and all that, I waded in and smashed my fist into his mouth.

Blood was everywhere, and panic erupted. His so-called mates soon pissed off, and I was left to face the bouncers again. The fact that the bar man was a big guy, and he was *sparko* on the canvas, the security staff gave me a little respect and a wide berth. I quickly picked Nev up and made my way outside, readying myself for the next onslaught. As I crashed through the exit doors, as luck would have it another guy called Anthony, who also happened to be on our course, was just getting into his Fiesta. I hurriedly explained the situation we were in, and he agreed to drive us both home. What a first encounter…

Coming from a poor village in South Yorkshire as I did, the prospect of going to university, or poly-technic as it was then, was somewhat remote. Most of my mates left school at sixteen and went straight down the pit as a collier, or into British Steel as a fitter. Having put my foot in the water as far as the steel industry was concerned and found it to be mind-numbingly boring, poly was definitely for me. Here I could be a pseudo intellect as no one knew me or my background. I started acting like Julie Walters in 'Educating Rita', by wearing dresses and pretending that I used to be a hairdresser. Being slightly older than my fellow students certainly gave me an edge, and being streetwise elevated to a different level. I grew a moustache and started to exhibit myself as a Lech Walesa lookalike, who supported the Anti-Communist Social Movement in Poland. If the truth be known, I hadn't a clue what I was supporting but it seemed to impress the girls, and that's what really mattered to me at the time. By donning a 'Solidarity' tee shirt I was deemed a radical amongst my peers.

I've come to realise over the years that it pays to research your subject for more than five minutes before you commence trying to overwhelm your audience with verbal diarrhoea. My rhetoric was hot air with no substance. It was only the thick no-hopers who thought of me as a revolutionary; most others thought of me as an arsehole. I dropped the political front, and decided to get into body-building, which was more akin to my brain power.

Muscles and women go hand in hand, so it was the gym for me.

During one session of weight lifting, I noticed Neville enter the gymnasium dressed as the referee in the film 'Kes'. I was fascinated by the prospect Nev actually mixing with beefy guys pushing weights, as he was only seven stone wet through. A lot of the lads in the gym stopped abruptly at Nev's arrival, with mouths agog, stunned at this weakling's presence amongst them. What the hell was a mere boy doing associating himself with the Leeds musclemen? You could feel the laughter ready to emanate from the bully-boys at Nev's tiny frame.

"Hey guys move over and let the dog see the rabbit. Allow me to show you how to use the bench-press. Watch what 'Atom-Ant' can shift," Nev said, convincing his ensemble of his superhuman strength.

I must admit, even I was taken aback at such a bold statement, considering the meat-heads in the gym. The one thing I came to realise about Nev was his total belief in his ability; a confidence that could have taken him to the top, even if this confidence was totally misplaced. Nev strutted over to where the bench machine was situated, clumsily knocking a chap out of the way in the process. The guy was so transfixed with Neville's apparent aura that he instantly forgave him, and like the rest of us was fascinated by what was about to unfold.

Nev steadied himself on the bench and shuffled rather awkwardly, whilst trying to adopt the correct posture to raise the barbell. His scrawny little body looked hopelessly out of proportion to the weights he was about to lift. I suggested that he ought to limber up first, and maybe take a few weights off either side of the bar. Arnold Schwarzenegger had previously been lifting them, such was the tonnage of the metal discs.

"No need for that matey-boy. I'm a lot stronger than I look. Lifting weights is all in the mind. Now look and learn," he quipped.

The tension was building, and you could have heard a pin drop. Nev, now settled into position on the bench-press, gripped the bar tightly. The old barbell presses were dangerous when lifting free weights, and didn't have any safety mechanism built in. When bench-pressing barbells, you had to have a buddy to be on standby in case of an accident. I stepped in and offered my services.

"No need for that, now move out of my way. This feels a tad light but let's go," was Nev's rebuke to me.

Unbelievably, he managed to lift the barbell and weights out of the metal safety jaws. This in itself was amazing, and I began to think that what Nev had been boasting about was going to prove all the 'Doubting Thomases' in the room wrong. Could he possibly press such a colossal amount of weight? The answer was immediate. The second the barbell was free of its housing it came crashing down onto Nev's throat, landing directly onto his Adam's apple, propelling the orb on a downwards journey to meet up with his testicles. The sheer force of the bars descent nearly decapitated him in the process. His tongue shot out like that of a serpent and Nev's face went instantly purple. His entire body went limp and I heard what distinctly sounded like a lamb being castrated with a blunt instrument.

Me and another guy rushed to his rescue and removed the bar from across his gullet. Neville was now lifeless and his tongue seemed to have grown twelve inches; it was drooping down the side of his face like a dog's when it's knackered. After several minutes he miraculously came round, much to everyone's relief. Even though we all knew inside that this feat of power from such a weedy guy was never going to materialise, we all admired the utter and complete confidence and belief that he held. Nev talked a good game, but unfortunately didn't play one.

Neville kindly offered to drive me into poly late one morning in his new car. He was very frugal with his money and unlike most students who ended up with massive overdrafts at the end of each term, had managed to save up enough *spendulics* and purchased a Chrysler Alpine. I was well chuffed for him, and the thought of a lift to college every day was wonderful. We did haggle about what he was intending to charge me and eventually settled on ten pence less than the price of my daily bus fare. Nev was no fool when it came to money.

As we drove towards the crossroads at Hyde Park on the way into poly, I suddenly became aware of a policeman in the middle of the road; I subsequently realised that the traffic lights were inoperable and it was his job to direct the traffic. Nev was busy rattling on about something or other and seemed totally oblivious to the policeman, and the imminent danger that he was about to subject him to.

"Neville, watch out for the copper in the road!" I screamed.

At that point we clipped the policeman with the driver's side wing mirror, and sent him spiralling off into the path of an oncoming ice-cream van. Thank goodness the driver of this vehicle had factored into his driving the potential problem looming, and managed to divert his van onto the pavement, sparing the bobby any further injury, but inadvertently turning his vehicle on its side, emptying its contents in the process.

"What kind of fucking idiot stands in the road waving his arms about like a demented chicken? That's the second time this morning I've hit him. You'd think he'd have learnt his lesson the first time," Nev said, cool as a cucumber.

I was utterly gobsmacked at what I'd just been privy to, astounded that Nev hadn't realised the gravity of his actions in nearly killing the policeman. In a state of shock, I said nothing more until we arrived at college. Nev's didn't bat an eyelid, and his apparent killing spree was laid to rest, like the poor policeman.

Having downed too many beers in the Subway and IPod public house one cold November evening, Nev and I stumbled home over the railway bridge towards our residence on Stanmore Place. We were definitely the worse for drink and couldn't make it home without having a pee-stop. Like a pair of inebriated oafs we fell into a garden hedge, giggling like school girls. Struggling to right ourselves, Nev in his wisdom opted to force his way through the privet hedge into the adjacent garden.

Bleary-eyed and half-cocked, he began to relieve himself on what he thought was a dwarf bush. It was only when the bush moved, and then growled he knew he was in deep trouble. The unsuspecting bush turned out to be a large Doberman, who happened to be chained up to a long leash, whose job was guarding the property from burglars and piss-artists. To say the dog was slightly miffed was somewhat of an understatement.

"Alf, what do I do? There's a great big bleeding dog here about to have me for supper," Nev whimpered to me.

Assessing the situation from the comfort of the other side of the hedge, I suggested that he take three steps backwards, then bend down, pick some shit up and throw it straight at the dog's face.

"What happens if there's no shit when I bend down?" he said to me.

"Don't worry mate," I replied, "If the dog is advancing on you, there will be!"

One of Neville's greatest escapes was his battle with the electric meter in the cellar. Being poor students and spending our entire paltry grant on ale and kebabs, no money was ever left over to pay the utility bills. A friend of mine had taken care of the gas for us, by disconnecting the meter and turning it upside down before reconnecting it; this enabled the meter to go backwards so we never paid any bills.

The electric proved more difficult, until our next door neighbour informed us how to bypass the meter, using a six-core length of wire approximately three feet long. This concept proved bloody marvellous but was extremely dangerous and highly illegal, and connecting the cable had to be accomplished with expert timing and precision. To ensure that we didn't get rumbled we fixed five different locks to the back door, and six to the front; it was easier to get access to Fort Knox. We also had a special secret knock to gain entry, such was our foolproof system. For added security we had all the bills put in the name of a fictitious Mr. Sergunda, who supposedly resided in the basement.

One lazy Saturday morning we heard a loud knock at the front door and back door simultaneously. I peered out of the skylight from my bedroom and immediately recognised the men from the Yorkshire Electricity Board in their blue uniforms, armed with an entry warrant. I quickly alerted the other guys from their respective beds, and our pre-arranged strategy of removing the cable kicked in. One guy was deployed to the back door, whilst another was sent to the front. Both parties pretended to have mislaid the keys in order to buy precious time in removing our wire from the meter and hiding it. The removal was pretty straightforward; one hand either side of it, coupled with a well timed yank usually did the trick. On this day though all didn't quite go to plan.

We managed to stall the YEB chaps with relative ease. Oh yes they hammered at both doors and shouted threats and demands, but we acted thick, like most students do. Slowly and methodically we released each lock, whilst the officials protested with great gusto. As I was unlocking the final latch on the back door, the house shook and rocked with a loud dull thud.

"What the fuck was that?" whispered Spider, one of the house-mates.

"I'm buggered if I know," I replied.

"Where's Nev?" cried Albert.

"He's on cable duty," I said.

"Oh bollocks!" we said in unison.

At that, the men from the YEB burst through the doors. They issued me with a summons, which I gratefully accepted on behalf of Mr. Sergunda, who happened to be on vacation. Storming towards the cellar doors, my thoughts immediately focused on Nev, and the fact that he hadn't appeared from the basement. Whipping the cable out was a two-second job, and poking it through the hole in the wall into next door's cellar was all of three seconds, totalling five seconds. He'd been missing for what seemed like an eternity.

The men in blue galloped down the staircase into the basement, with me quickly in pursuit. Scanning the room I noticed that the cable had fortunately been removed from the meter housing. The officials started making threats to me about how long I would be incarcerated, but I wasn't really paying any attention to them as I was too preoccupied searching for Neville. The basement was pretty big, with a selection of loose weights and various weight training machines. There was also a large bundle of collapsed cardboard boxes and a pile of old clothes.

No matter how hard I looked for poor old Nev, he was nowhere to be seen. He couldn't possibly vanish into thin air, so where the bloody hell was he? Without drawing any undue attention to myself I started to move the boxes, pretending to be searching for my dumbbells. Having restacked all the cardboard there was still no sign of my buddy. Meanwhile, the YEB men had placed a secure wire cage around our electric meter, and littered the adjoining walls with stickers warning occupants of illegal tampering, etc. I still couldn't bring myself to listen to the wittering arseholes about my impending jail sentence; for some strange reason they thought that I was Sergunda.

As I bent down to move a stray garment from the floor I heard a faint murmur coming from the far end of the cellar, behind the stack of old clothes. Albert and Spider had now joined us in the cellar, giving me a little room to manoeuvre my way to the rear of the basement to ascertain the noise I heard. Pulling back a large poncho I was amazed to discover Neville, laying face down not moving. Shit, I thought, I hope the silly bugger isn't dead. I leant over to touch him and to my horror received an electric shock; he was oozing electricity.

To distract the meter men I kicked Nev and told him to get up, making merriment, saying that he was feigning sleep to get out of the housework. They were so transfixed with their meter housing that they ignored my actions. Spider started waffling on to them about Mr. Sergunda, so I saw this as my opportunity to rouse Nev from the dead. As luck would have it he opened his eyes and yawned.

"What the hell happened to me Alf?" he groggily murmured.

Grabbing the now conscious Neville by his shoes, I helped him to the bottom of the stairwell and he slowly managed to get to his feet. I assisted him up several flights of stairs into my bedroom, and sat him down on the bed.

"Are you alright mate?" I said.

"No not really. I remember what happened now. When I pulled the cable out it didn't come out in one piece. One end stayed in the electrical supply whilst the other end touched the metal bullworker hanging up. The next thing I recall was a large blue flash, the smell of burning and me flying through the air. I must have crashed into the wall knocking myself out. Thank God I landed in the soft pile of clothes," he replied.

"Well at least you are okay now pal. When I tried moving you I got a shock. You were still full of electricity for some reason," I went on to say.

"Well that's how they brought Frankenstein to life, isn't it?" he answered.

Neville was a smashing bloke and I still miss him terribly. He died young overseas, and the world lost a true gem. With all his idiosyncrasies and odd-ball behaviour, Nev was a true mate, a trusted friend and colleague. He still possesses the knack of making me laugh when I recall our adventures together. What I'd give now for him to be still here with me. Somewhere in heaven, he will be wreaking havoc in his special way, telling all the inhabitants what a brilliant snooker player he is.

Chapter 24
U. S. of A. (Part One)

As I neared the end of my first year at Leeds Polytechnic in May 1982, my mate Smig cajoled me into attending an interview in London for a placement in the United States of America. The previous year had taken Smig to Maryland working for BUNAC (British Universities North America Club). For twelve months he had bored me rigid with his stories about how the American girls were gagging for sex with British guys, and how many conquests he'd carried out over there, furthering the special relationship Britain has with the USA. It sounded pretty reasonable to me, so I decided to try it on for size.

The interviews were held in the capital so we travelled down by train to Russell Square for the formal interrogation; I had been recommended by Smig so I managed to skip the preliminaries. During my trip down to London, I had to decide which subjects I would like to teach the American children. The idea was that you specialised in one particular subject and one subsidiary subject. Checking out the blurb I'd been previously sent, I was delighted to see that photography and soccer—football to me and you—was on the list of proposed activities and subjects. I was a decent footie player and I'd been schooled in the art of photography by Mr. Norton in the scouts, so was quite adept. The interview was daunting to say the least, but I passed with flying colours—by basically lying through my back teeth about my achievements. When confronted with things I don't know or am uncomfortable with I tend to be creative with the truth and waffle a lot. That particular day, the interviewees were plentiful, so in my humble opinion I was only granted the contract due to tight time constraints.

Job in the bag, Smig and I then had to apply for a visa to get into America; this was a different ball game. No lying here as the American authorities were strict beyond belief. We had both forgotten about my criminal record. To enter America you had to tick all the boxes back then. If you'd been arrested for drugs, busted for firearm offences or grievous bodily harm, the chances of you getting your visa were next to nil. Luckily for me my previous charge of GBH had been dropped to ABH (actual bodily harm). I waited patiently outside the visa office for four hours before finally being accepted and having my visa granted. I was overwhelmed at this; it was like passing a maths exam. I honestly thought that I was going to be turned down, not because of my rap sheet, but because coming from Maltby was an offence in itself.

I took Smig for a celebratory beer and we ended up getting hammered and missed the last train home. We trawled around Soho for most of the night dreaming of sex. Back in the 1980s you could have a hand job from a prostitute for £5. For an extra quid she'd give you a complimentary bread cake. At about three in the morning, we clambered over a fence and slept in some ornamental park with a load of gay blokes—enough said.

Four weeks later, we were on our way over the pond on a jumbo jet. As I mentioned, I've never really liked flying, because of my fear of not being in control. To help me overcome my anxiety I got loaded on the outbound journey after being plied with free booze by a flirty air hostess. For seven hours whilst I was flying over the Atlantic to JFK Airport in New York, the only thing that I can vaguely recall is being asked to calm down or the pilot would have me removed from the plane; the prospect of being thrown off at thirty thousand feet quickly sobered me up.

When we finally landed in America the first thing that struck me was the intense humidity. I had never experienced anything like that before and I must admit that I felt uneasy and clammy. Sweating for no apparent reason seemed all together wrong. As I made my way through Customs, the thought of my criminal record haunted me. But I'd been issued my visa, so entering New York should have been a mere formality. I was laden down with a massive orange fluorescent rucksack and still semi-pissed from the free booze I'd consumed on the plane. Add to the mix a large dose of paranoia and I stood out like a drug mule, sweating profusely and acting rather strange. The strain was obvious even to a blind man, and I started to feel nauseous and dizzy.

"Welcome to the United States of America Alf," said a large black Customs lady.

Oh bollocks, I thought. They bloody know me. What chance have I got to get in now? Before I could answer, Smig tapped me on the shoulder and explained that my huge name tag dangling off the back of my rucksack was clearly visible for all to see. The lady had just used her initiative when addressing me in person. *Jesus wept,* was my instant reaction, and the feeling of total relief came over me like an orgasm. My false smile and nervous demeanour suddenly disappeared and the old me returned. Back then, all US Customs officials had a large, thick black book at their disposal, which resembled a family bible but read a lot more. A cursory flick through this book revealed whether or not you were a listed felon or hardened criminal. The lady in charge took a long deep look into my eyes and began to thumb through the pages. A startled expression again filled my face, and impending doom surged over me.

"I don't think I need to check you out Sir. You have an honest, caring face. Have a nice day," she said to me.

I was gobsmacked. Honest caring face; was she on drugs? Not one to look a gift horse in the mouth, I mumbled something inane and smiled at her. Smig nudged me in the arse and told me to get a move on.

Clambering into a yellow cab waiting outside the terminal I was still in a state of shock, but at least I was officially in America now. No sooner had we left the airport, the cab driver lit a spliff and handed it to me through his glass partition. Having just got through Customs by the skin of my teeth several minutes earlier and still a little shaken, I now found myself smoking grass in a taxi with a complete stranger, who turned out to be bloody Russian. I could see this trip being memorable, or *very* short.

The cabbie dropped us off at the YMCA in the centre of New York. Having helped my new comrade smoke his joint, I was feeling very mellow and laid back; I didn't give a shit whether or not the authorities threw me in the can now, such was my happy mood. I was on cloud twelve, having bypassed nine, ten and eleven. I do not advocate taking drugs in any way whatsoever, and whilst I'm writing this cannot believe I succumbed to marijuana so easily and quickly that day in the taxi. Maybe I was still traumatised from the thought of being arrested and chucked out of the States, or maybe I was simply young and stupid. It did, however, feel so normal though at that particular time.

After checking into the accommodation, me and Smig hooked up with a few English guys we had met on the plane and it was off to nearest bar. We'd only walked a couple of blocks before we found an Irish bar called O'Tooles, and the idea of sinking a pint of Guinness or three whetted our appetites. As I opened the rickety wooden entrance door, a beefy Irishman firmly gripped my shoulder and asked for ID. At the time I was twenty-one and sporting a beard of sorts. Why did he think I was underage? He made us all produce our passports before allowing us in. Sitting at the bar I ordered a pint of the black stuff, but I was told the barrel had run out and would beer suffice. I was also asked to move away from the bar and take a seat at a nearby table. My initial impression of Irish/American hospitality was nil; the natives certainly didn't take an instant liking to us. When the beer arrived at the table it was in a large pitcher complete with a set of small glasses. Having examined the pitcher of beer, which seemed half beer, half froth, I ordered four more; one for each of us. Draught American beer was too fizzy and weak for my liking, and after drinking eight pints I found myself being poured out of the door by the beefy guy.

It was now beginning to get dark and we decided to make our back to the hostel. To say the YMCA was basic was an understatement; even the cockroaches didn't stay there. If you ever get the chance to spend a night in one be prepared; take a gun, a bodyguard, never go into the showers alone, cement your arsehole up, and don't sleep with the door open. If I thought the humidity was bad during the daytime, it was stifling at night; I struggled to breathe and felt unclean. I shared a room with a guy called Derek Heap, and to help keep cool, I stupidly wedged the bedroom open as well as the window to create a breeze.

No sooner had we got into our beds, some axe-murdering psychotic lunatic calmly walked into the room brandishing a knife and a massive hard-on. Initially I thought that I was having a flash-back from the weed I'd smoked earlier, but when the deranged pervert started to get into bed with me, I suddenly realised that my back passage was never going to be the same size again. Derek jumped to my rescue and knocked the guy flying into the wall, and then he grabbed my arm and dragged me into the corridor. We ran for our lives down to reception some six floors below. When we explained what had happened to the night porter, he simply laughed and said,

"Oh that's old Jack who came into your room. He's harmless. He only wants someone to talk to. Did you by any chance leave the door ajar?"

Fucking harmless? He had a knife and a raging hard-on. "I don't think he had a conversation on his mind, just frenzied sex," I answered.

"Calm down sir, I'll go and retrieve him and escort him back to his room," the porter replied.

"What about the knife?" I asked, all concerned.

"It's not a knife sir, it's a vibrator," the porter said still laughing.

"Oh that's alright then. Lucky me; he just wanted to butt-fuck me with both his weapons. How charming," I sarcastically replied.

The porter shuffled off to reunite the stray with his room. Derek and I decided to crash in Smig's room, and that night we both slept upright, bound in the bed clothes like a mummy, with one eye open, for fear of being gang raped, or being eaten alive by Hannibal Lecter.

The following morning we headed off to Thurmont, in the state of Maryland, on a Greyhound bus. I was shattered from the previous night's high jinks and bedroom antics, and nodded off, missing all the magnificent scenery along the route. Several hours later we arrived at our destination; Camp Hairy. We were met at the gates by the head of the camp, a Jewish gentleman called Isaac Hunt. He explained about what was expected of us, and that the summer camp was only for Jewish American children. Being a newcomer I was classed as a 'counsellor at large' and assigned to act as support to a group of delinquent, bed-wetting, filthy rich brats. No, that's unfair; only one was a bed-wetter, and he ended up being my co-counsellor.

The setting of Camp Hairy was awesome; surrounded by dense woodland and fields, wooden shacks in the centre. There was an outdoor swimming pool, a large restaurant hall, two fishing ponds, and an indoor arena. The one thing that totally blew my mind was the enormous scale of the site; it was vast. For the first few days we settled into the new routine that was Camp Hairy. Having been a scout, this seemed like second nature to me, only this time we were sleeping in log cabins, and not under smelly canvas.

After three days I was promoted to Counsellor and along with my robotic buddy Dirk, allotted ten kids to look after, 24/7. Dirk was off the human scale all together; he spoke in words of only one syllable, showered naked in his hiking boots, had a 'Prince Albert' in his male appendage, which apparently used to belong to his granny, and tried to convince me that in a previous life he was a crop circle. From our initial meeting, I just knew we'd get along champion. Dirk told me he was a strict Mormon; I may have misheard him, because having got to know him quite well over a period of eight weeks I think what he meant to say was "thick moron".

Dirk was also an avid reader of pornographic literature, hence his thick spectacles and endless supply of tissues. He didn't relate to children at all, and why he was actually there I found somewhat bewildering. His specialist subject was astronomy, and his sport was wrestling. I wondered whether or not he'd want to wrestle naked with the kids or just make them shower with him in their hiking boots. He was relatively harmless, and left me in charge of my little troop, which suited me fine.

Getting to know the kids in my care was great. Firstly I told them that I was a Falklands vet, and had killed fifty men in combat; this put fear straight up them. I went on to say that I was also a disciplinarian who opted for a zero tolerance policy on just about everything. The final piece in my wicked jigsaw of outright lies was to inform them that they were now in my platoon, under my strict command. Everything that I ordered them to do had to be done double-sharp, without question. Amazingly, my terrified ensemble all agreed to my demands.

The 'F' Troop as they were christened was comprised of a bunch of young boys, whose parents had too much money and too little quality time to spend with their loved ones; they knew the price of everything, and the value of nothing. Coming from poor stock I struggled to comprehend the extent of their wealth and felt sorry for the kids as they seemed to lack love and real attention in their lives. Some of the parents didn't even have the decency to say goodbye, let alone give their offspring a hug or a kiss when dropping them off. It was a case of

"Here's my kids, look after them for a month or two."

The kids all put on a brave face as their respective parents zoomed down the long driveway, homeward bound. I remember standing there watching this surreal episode; these kids were only ten years old for Christ sake. I could feel the hurt in their eyes as they pretended that they didn't care also. It was heartbreaking to witness. As the last overweight, insensitive parent bid me farewell, whilst neglecting to acknowledge his/her child, I rounded up my lads and made them sit in a circle, like the native North American Indians used to do. I explained to them that this was going to be an education in life for them that they would never forget. After all, their parents had paid a lot of dollars for them to be there, and they had the pleasure of having me to look forward to for the next two months, which was a blessing in itself.

I've always found relating to kids and young adolescents easy; I try to see it from their perspective and listen attentively when they are speaking to me. Kids need a role model to look up to, and need nurturing and motivating to enable them to realise their true potential. They also need discipline; not good hidings and the likes, but more structure. They need to understand cause and effect, and proper values. Young people learn at different speeds, and I've always maintained that if you make teaching interesting and funny so the pupils can actually relate to it, and all feel part of the learning process, you're halfway to doing your job correctly. Kids and parents need to comprehend that respect is earned, and should never be taken for granted. If this fails, just ignore everything I've just spouted on about, and beat the crap out of the little fuckers; the birch never did me any harm!

My time at the camp flew by. I quickly learned all the scams and tricks that the kids got up to, and taught them a lot more they didn't know. I also realised that vetting all the kids' mail before it was sent home enabled me to somewhat embellish my particular attributes and what a superb counsellor I was. I took it upon myself to have the kids rewrite vast swathes of their mail, prior to posting, so the letters would read much better and make me seem like a great guy. It worked a treat and after the first month I was inundated with massive tips from the parents of my troop, which helped supplement my meagre wage. Being a decent sort of crook, for my scam to come off, I allowed all the kids under my wing to read Dirk's porn; they seemed content with the arrangement, so it was happy days all round.

Looking after kids week on week is certainly no easy task. The onus of responsibility laid on your shoulders is immense. Back then it was arduous; Lord only knows what it would be like now, what with the claims-culture that surrounds us all and the responsibility with being around and involved with young kids. Common sense fortunately pre-vailed, and the kids got treated in a correct and dignified manner. On one occasion, however, I did question the camp leader about his methods, and this was the start of my downfall.

My kids had won some competition or other, so I agreed that they could have a midnight candy feast as a treat. However, during dinner that evening the camp commandant informed everyone that several younger kids had played a practical joke on the camp nurse, causing her deep upset, so he declared that all the children would be confined to bunks as a punishment. I found this disgraceful, and told him so. It had nothing whatsoever to do with my particular kids, so in my humble opinion he was well out of order. It was ironic that in a Jewish camp, kids were being punished for a crime that they didn't commit; his words were, "The innocent must suffer with the guilty."

What a crock of shit; being part Jewish, if only a small part, I again confronted him on the issue and said that I wasn't prepared to go along with his rules as they seemed somewhat anti-Semitic to me, and that my kids were having their treat as I'd promised. Discrimination can take many forms. This didn't go down too well, and I was summoned to a meeting that night and threatened with dismissal. I remember listening to the guy's rhetoric and the reasoning behind his demands and thinking to myself, what a wanker. I shook my head in mock disagreement whilst saying yes, and marched out back to my cabin. After lights out, I waited one hour, then got the kids up and let them have their celebratory candy. Next morning I was back for further interrogation and a severe reprimand. I was warned by my fellow campers that I was on my way out of Camp Hairy.

Chapter 25
U. S. of A. (Part Two)

Still pretty pissed off about being summoned to explain myself yet again to the camp leader, I was astonished to find him in a receptive mood. The previous night, this guy could have got on the Archbishop of Canterbury's tits, however, this morning he appeared calm and reasonable. Incredibly he apologised for his actions and shook my hand, telling me, "Let's learn from this and move on." I was pretty dumbstruck about the entire sordid episode, but I accepted his apology and moved on.

That evening, by way of a celebration, I went for a few beers with my English buddy Darren and my new American chum Dan. Darren was a 'James Dean' lookalike who had a wicked sense of humour; Dan was built like 'Sly Stallone', and didn't possess any sense of humour. We drove into the nearby town of Thurmont and visited the legendary Jewish pub, the 'Bar Mitzvah'. It was full of chicks who seemed to love the British accent and all that went with it. No sooner had I sat down when a girl approached me and said,

"What's five feet two, winks and fucks like a rabbit?"

"I have no idea," was my feeble reply.

The girl in question winked at me and walked away smiling to herself. *Bingo*, I thought, that'll do for me Tommy. I followed her to the bar, where she proceeded to fill a glass up with ice cubes.

"Have you ever had a Mexican blow-job?" she whispered.

I hadn't a clue what a Mexican blow-job was, but when she filled her mouth with ice and led me by the hand outside, I soon got the picture. During this very quick experience, all I could think about was the night-cap that I used to drink when I was a bartender in Jersey, which was a *Baileys with ice*. After the initiation ceremony, my new friend took one look at my manhood and said that I wasn't cut out to be a Jew, and gave me her Baltimore Oriels baseball cap as a gift; I couldn't believe my luck. Smig was actually telling the truth for a change. After an hour or so we left the bar, and drove over to our sister camp which was known as Camp Mot. They were having a *par-tay*.

Another guy had now joined us, called John, who brought along with him a case of Pabst Blue Ribbon beer for the journey. We all crammed into John's Ford Capri, which he had just purchased that morning. He asked me if I'd ever driven a stick-shift. I didn't understand his question until I realised he meant a car with a gear stick; American cars were all automatic. This was no problem for me as stick-shift cars were all I'd ever driven back in the UK. The fact that I was three parts pissed from the beer should have alerted me to the danger I was getting us all into.

But I was young and delinquent back then, and the thought of all the young chicks sleeping alone at our sister camp, fuelled my passion for rampant sex, so off we roared, down 'Vagina Highway' to rendezvous with our damsels in waiting.

Having arrived at Camp Mot the worse for wear and full of Dutch courage, we embarked on a series of tormenting the nubile fillies, by flirting outrageously with them whilst touching them up. They didn't seem to mind the groping, and one thing soon led to another. I became detached from our group as my brain became detached from my body, and my cock took over. To cut a long story short, I was caught in a compromising position, sand-wiched naked between twins dressed as nurses.

The cordial meeting I'd had with Isaac Hunt the previous day was a million miles away from the one the next morning, following the disclosure of my indiscretions at Camp Mot. Isaac blew a gas-ket and fired me on the spot; I was the first British counsellor to be canned from Camp Hairy in seven-teen years. The gravity of my situation, the fact that I had no money, nowhere to stay, just two weeks before my contract officially ended hit me hard. What was I going to do?

Fortunately, my new buddy Dan stepped in and invited me to stay at his house. Dan and I were escorted off the camp grounds by two armed guards, drafted in from nearby Camp David. The guards were pretty cool with us and bid us farewell at the gates. As a final gesture of goodwill, Isaac gave me twenty dollars which somewhat surprised me. He then reminded me of the fact that I had been well ahead of the rest of the field in the camp competi-tion, 'Counsellor of the Year' but alas now wouldn't win it.

Leaving the camp behind was really sad for me, as I'd made some great mates and new acquaintances, especially the children under my care. I was told afterwards that all the kids from my troop wore black armbands that evening at the lowering of the American flag, as a mark of respect for me, and defiance against the camp leader. They were then all punished by having their candy treats stopped for a week; Darren said not one of them complained.

Arriving at Dan's house in Potomac, Washington DC, I was overwhelmed by the size and interior decor; it exuded opulence and wealth. His parents were both professional people and the house reflected their status in American society. When I realised that the family owned five cars I was flabbergasted. They also had five bedrooms and a basement bigger than my house, complete with all the modern trimmings, including a juke box and a pool table. I'd never before experienced such affluence, and in all honesty, it was too much to take in all in one go.

Dan, having been brought up in this lavish, palatial environment, thought nothing of it and took it all in his stride. He lied to his parents about why we were both there, and made me feel at home immediately. What struck me about my friendship with Dan was that we'd only known each other a couple of days, and this didn't seem to matter at all to him. Here he was, allowing me to stay at his folks' house, all expenses paid, and wanted nothing in return. To say that Dan was a top bloke was an understatement.

I was allocated the basement, complete with my own bedroom, bathroom with shower, and bidet; I had never seen a bidet in a house before and found myself ill at ease with this porcelain bum wash. I was used to wiping my arse on newspaper, not having a colonic irrigation. Another thing that blew me away was air conditioning. It hadn't been invented in the UK back then, and I had the privilege of it in a cellar!

After I'd settled in and dumped my bags, Dan's mum summoned me to a meeting on their outside deck. She'd had the foresight to have telephoned Camp Hairy, and had actually spoken to Isaac Hunt about mine and Dan's dismissal. The thing that pissed her off was the fact we lied to her; she didn't give a shit about us getting fired. I smoothed things over with my best English accent, and offered to cut the lawns, but only after we'd had afternoon tea, which I insisted on making. It did the trick and I was accepted into Dan's household.

That evening over supper, Dan's parents informed us that they intended taking a trip to Niagara Falls, and asked if we would like to join them. Before I'd had chance to say anything, Dan winked at me and turned them down flat. The following morning, his parents disappeared for three weeks, and we were left home alone. No sooner had their car vanished from the cul-de-sac, Dan was on the horn to his buddies, who must have already been hiding outside in the garden, such was their immediate entry through the front door. Armed with beer and drugs, the party was in full swing in seconds. I just went with the flow, and woke up three weeks later in rehab. On a serious note, it was mind-blowing in every sense of the word; girls, booze, dope, and more girls. For me, it was like being a pop star. I couldn't believe my luck. The curse that my ancestry had placed on me was finally being vanquished. Things were definitely looking up.

After several days of giving the 'ball a kick', we finally ventured outside and went to a nearby bar in downtown DC. Firstly I insisted we take a detour and visit Georgetown, so I could see the steps that featured in the finale of the 'Exorcist' where the possessed priest meets a gruesome end. This film epitomises everything a horror movie should be; believable, terrifying, different and leaving you numb with fear for days afterwards. I still think that it is the greatest horror flick of all time. Considering it was released in 1973, and dealt with demonic possession of a child, the movie broke new grounds in being shit-scared. I love this film with the same passion I love 'Kes'; both movies have had a profound impact on my life.

Having walked down the steps from where the house was situated, to the bottom of the road where the demonic priest died, I was horrified to see Dan taking a piss on the steps. This was a cardinal sin in my book and an argument erupted between the pair of us. He couldn't understand my feelings for this particular film location, and I couldn't be arsed to explain it to the philistine.

After our fiery altercation, we ventured into an Irish bar for more amber nectar. It was strange to witness people collecting for Noraid, an Irish American fund raising organisation, mainly for the IRA. Back in Maltby, we struggled to collect raffle ticket money; such was the tightness and poverty of its inhabitants. We downed a few *sherbets* and staggered back to the car. By the time I had squeezed myself into the back seat, along with eight other drunkards, the smell of marijuana inside the car was overpowering; several of the passengers had lit up, and with the car windows firmly shut, you couldn't see the end of your nose such was the dense smoke. We had only travelled fifty yards before we were pulled over by the police.

As one of the officers moved towards the driver's door, the ensuing pandemonium inside the vehicle hit fever pitch. People were eating joints like they were chips. Todd, our driver, gingerly opened the door and a great plume of smoke resembling a mushroom cloud from an atom bomb explosion ascended into the night sky. The officer at the scene then uttered the immortal words,

"Hey guys, have you been smoking marijuana?"

"Fucking hell, it's Sherlock Holmes," I sarcastically replied.

At this the police officer yanked me from the back seat and bounced me off the side of the car. He then spun me round and made me 'spread-eagle' across the car's bonnet. To assist me in opening my legs wider he rattled my inner knee caps with his baton. The pain was horrendous and I collapsed onto the tarmac. A swift kick to my rear up righted me quickly, and once again I assumed the position, but correctly this time. He then proceeded to read me the riot act, saying that because I was British, I wouldn't get any leniency from him, only more punishment. I immediately tendered my apologies and referred to him as Sir.

The accompanying officer joined him at our vehicle and Todd was given a breath test. If you have never seen an American breath test, click on YouTube and watch in total amazement. If it wasn't for the pain I was suffering from my shattered knees and the prospect of being hurled into a Washington DC slammer by Robocop, I would have pissed my sides. It was sheer comedy to observe. Todd was requested to recite the alphabet backwards, whilst standing on one leg. At the same time he was instructed to connect his index finger with the end of his nose, and walk in a straight line, whistling 'Dixie'. Todd failed all the set tasks and was heavily fined. I was confined to a wheelchair for a week, but it was well worth it, such was the fiasco.

One afternoon we decided to have a mini road trip to Baltimore, where Dan and I arranged to meet up with Smig and a few chums. We visited the notorious 'Block,' the equivalent to Hamburg's Reeperbahn, the city centre's red light district. We clumsily rocked up at a strip joint and sat in a line at the bar, like dogs waiting to be fed; tongues hanging out, panting for nourishment. Men are pathetic when it comes to brothels or lap dancing venues, as they start acting like teenagers, showing off, being loud and obnoxious, but underneath shitting themselves.

The bar servery was circular with an inner back fitting doubling as a stage. Having ordered a beer and finding out it cost more than a new car I began to get ready to do a runner; that was until the first stripper appeared from behind a red velvet curtain adjacent the bar. Her introduction went like this,

"She's not got a 48 inch bust. She's not got a 58 inch bust. Yes folks, you've guessed it, Tiffany has got a 68 inch pair of hooters."

It ranks as one of the best intro's I've ever heard. To top it off, she waltzed up to the small elevated stage, carrying two empty metal dustbins wedged under each breast. The sight of these gigantic hooters and two dustbins still haunts me to this day; I would have struggled picking the pair of them up with my hands. The bins that is, not her tits.

On seeing this magnificent feat of strength, Smig jumped from his bar stool straight over the counter and onto Tiffany, declaring at the top of his voice his undying love for her. Within seconds he was pounced on from all sides by six black gladiators who kicked the shit out of him. Normally I would have gone to his rescue, but I was totally transfixed by Tiff's massive orbs. Even though she was in her seventies with no teeth to speak of, those fun bags were truly awe inspiring. She could have breast fed an army and still had plenty left over. The rest of that night's shows were somewhat of a letdown after Tiffany's wonderful performance. One beautiful black stripper gave me her number inside a pair of knickers, which was a first for me. Yes I was tempted, but having paid for one drink, found myself bankrupt for the remainder of the evening. I still have the prized panties she gave me, and wear them when my wife's not looking.

During my brief stay at Camp Hairy I was fortunate enough to play against the famous soccer team 'Baltimore Blast'. It was a unique experience for me because as we left the field, having drawn five all, spectators besieged us for our autographs. I remember standing there with a bunch of young adolescents begging me to sign their programmes. It was totally weird. Obviously the professional American sportsmen duly obliged as it was the custom. For us Brits it was overwhelming; I now know how David Beckham must feel every time he ventures outside. When penning my moniker on the kids' programmes, I wrote personal messages that would mean something special. Things like, "All the best you set of wankers", and "Best wishes you bollock heads", as was my childish sense of humour.

Dan and I had many more adventures together and carried out some dastardly deeds with young *Japs*—Jewish American Princesses—all in the name of furthering the special bond that our two countries share. Drinking champagne from stilettos; creating our own version of *Casey Jones* on the girl from Illinois; getting arrested in Kentucky; having a knife pulled on me in Washington; waking up naked in a forest somewhere in Maryland handcuffed, and me being the first English counsellor to get the chop from Camp Hairy.

I travelled quite extensively during my brief visit to the USA; I visited New York, Pennsylvania, Virginia, North Carolina, South Carolina, Georgia, Kentucky, and Tennessee. I met and stayed with some fantastic friends, namely, Dan Grimley, John Epstein, Pepe, Alan Rhinestein, Eric Tupton, Marti Goss, Dave Sadagore, Steve Ratcliffe, Todd Cecil, Todd Carty (oh sorry, he was in 'EastEnders' and

'The Bill').

My time in America was fleeting and I would love to scribe an entire book about my exploits there. The unfortunate thing about my short but illustrious stay is that I can't remember much about it; this has everything to do with the fact that I was either permanently inebriated, stoned, or both.

It is difficult to describe America to someone who hasn't been there. The people are generally excellent; they are positive and forthright. They will help build you up and put you on a pedestal. If you fall off, for whatever reason, they will pick you up, brush you down, and put you back up, such is their genuine desire for encouraging people to achieve success. They are a nation of squad players; being in a squad for them is as good as being in the first team. They like to be part of something.

Trying to wax lyrical about this great nation, or think up superlatives is a waste of time. All the great and good have said it all before. To me, the best word which describes America and its people is simply 'awesome'. Pardon me, I meant to say 'awful'. No more blowing up your soft Yankee ass.

Remember Big Brother, without the cooperation and allegiance of the Brits, you wouldn't have fucked up half as much in Iraq and Afghanistan. You must accept that when the world and his dog loathe and despise you, simply remember that laughter is the best medicine. Learn to laugh at yourself, everybody else does.

It is also worth noting that my first novel only sold three copies when it was published over there, and believe me, it is wickedly-pisser-funny. Have you no sense of humour? Oh I'm sorry, I forgot; that's right, you haven't!

Flying back to dear old England was a complete blur to me. Several days later I was still suffering from jet-lag and struggling to function properly. One morning I awoke from a heavy sleep to find something on my pillow that shocked me to the bone; the curse of Alf had struck with a vengeance.

What was this curse, I hear you say? You'll have to wait for the next instalment…stay tuned folks.

A Note on Names and People

Up to the age of seventeen, my late Grandad supplied me with a vast amount of background information and opinion, all of which I implicitly believed to be true, therefore I have subsequently written what I was told, never questioning his wisdom and rhetoric. From the age of seventeen until I reached the "key of the door" milestone, my late Uncle Tony became my mentor and advisor, and like Grandad, I believed every word he told me. My friends names have all been mixed up with that of friends from later years, swapped around somewhat, and spiced up to create fictionalized individuals. The descriptions of these people are merged with traits and idiosyncrasies from other people I have had the good fortune to meet in my life, but the actual events are true, but not necessarily in the same true order. Where real forenames and nick-names are used, the specific events relating to these individuals are a mixture of fact and fiction.

About the Author

Dene Lindley is the author of one rather amusing book, *Unlucky Alf*. His pathetic life has been beset with misfortunes and bad luck. Added to this, he is blessed with being a bipolar depressive which means he swings both ways with bears whilst remaining miserable. His Headmaster described him as useless to the entire school assembly, and said that it was "… a waste of time trying to polish a turd." This kind of encouragement helped Dene enormously, and contributed to his low self-esteem, habitual nose-picking and an unhealthy obsession for gurning at ginger headed people. His wife is constantly challenged by his mood swings and cross-dressing. Life is never dull when you are around Dene, but he does have a tendency to poke people in the eye for no apparent reason, and then giggle hysterically. He would like to dedicate this book to bald men and bean-flickers.

Lightning Source UK Ltd.
Milton Keynes UK
21 November 2009
146544UK00001B/1/P